TEACH YOURSELF BOOKS
NEW TESTAMENT GREEK

D0863618

For the student who wants to get up New Testament Greek this is admirable as a beginning. The exercises and vocabularies are very well chosen and, unlike most of these books, the overall impression is that the dreary grammar is kept down to a minimum and the student is encouraged as soon as possible to find the New Testament for himself.

Dr. William Neil

NEW TESTAMENT GREEK

D. F. Hudson

Long-renowned as the authoritative source for self-guided learning – with more than 30 million copies sold worldwide – the *Teach Yourself* series includes over 200 titles in the fields of languages, crafts, hobbies, sports, and other leisure activities.

A Catalogue for this title is available from the British Library

Library of Congress Catalog Card Number: 92-82507

First published in UK 1992 by Hodder Headline Plc, 338 Euston Road, London NW1 3BH

First published in US 1993 by NTC Publishing Group, 4255 West Touhy Avenue, Lincolnwood (Chicago), Illinois 60646 – 1975 U.S.A.

Printed in Great Britain by Cox & Wyman Ltd, Reading, Berkshire.

Impression number	14	13	12	11	10	9	8	7	6
Year		1999	1998	1997	1996				

PREFACE

Some years ago an Englishman who was teaching New Testament Greek to Indian students and a Norwegian who was teaching it to Chinese students compared notes about method, and summed up the conversation in two words— " Bully them ! " This book may be said to have arisen from that conversation, since there is clearly something wrong when keen young men who have a vocation for the Christian ministry have to be bullied into an essential part of the preparation of it. Two things are obvious about the standard grammars of New Testament Greek—first that they are dull, and secondly that the English is usually " biblical ". Even in Britain it is now realized that the language of the Authorized or Revised Versions is not understood by the modern pagan, and to Indian students it is almost a new language which they have to learn as a step to Greek. Further, it creates a subconscious impression that the language of the New Testament was archaic, which is the exact opposite of the truth. The present writer made a few experiments with exercises in modern English, but these were not very successful, and it was the discovery of the companion book in this series, *Teach Yourself Greek*, which brought a great hope that something similar might be done for New Testament Greek. The Classical book was useless after the first few lessons because of its completely different vocabulary, and because Hellenistic Greek has many peculiarities of its own, but a very sincere debt of gratitude must be recorded to the earlier book, which has provided the basic method of the present one, and also quite a number of illustrations. A number of colleagues in Indian theological colleges have been encouraging in their comments on the book, and particular thanks are due to my colleague in Serampore College, Mr. Mathew P. John, M.A., M.Th., who has himself used the course in an early form and made many helpful suggestions, and to Dr. Thomas Sitther, formerly Principal of the Tamilnad Theological College, Tirumaraiyur, whose long experience made his comments very valuable, whilst in Britain encouragement and helpful comments have been made by my former teacher, Dr. A. M. Hunter, and by Mr. H. Carey Oakley, M.A., who has carefully and constructively scrutinized the proofs. But perhaps the most important contribution to the book has been by the " guinea-pigs " in three successive classes of students who bore with the incompleteness of earlier drafts and were always very ready to point out misprints in the typescript! The fact that they learned enough to pass the examination encouraged the hope that the course was workable.

CONTENTS

NOTE ON METHOD

For the last thirty or forty years there has been a lot of argument about the method of teaching languages and much has been said in favour of the " Direct Method ". It is argued (and rightly) that the natural way to learn a language is the way by which a child learns its mother-tongue—by picking up the names of things, and by imitation. What is often forgotten is that no child is really fluent in its mother-tongue, which it hears spoken around it all the time, until it is in its teens. If, therefore, you can spend ten or a dozen years in an environment in which the language is spoken all the time, you can depend solely on the Direct Method! With Hellenistic Greek the question of environment is somewhat difficult until Mr. H. G. Wells' Time-machine becomes a reality, and in any case no one wants to spend ten or a dozen years learning it. Nor is it necessary, for the adult has powers of reasoning and co-ordination which can cut down the time of enabling him to grasp the general rules and principles which govern the grammar and syntax of a language. It is important, how-ever, to bear in mind that the power of reasoning *organizes* the work, but does not cut it out altogether, and it involves a certain amount of learning by rote the basic patterns of the language. This course has been worked out to cover a period of roughly twenty-eight weeks, spending about eight hours a week, by which time it should be possible to get a working knowledge of the Greek of the New Testament. The attempt has been made to make the course interesting, and even in places amusing, but there is no painless method of learning any language in half a dozen easy lessons, and it is most important that the declensions and conjugations, in particular, should be learned, and learned thoroughly, as they come. The schoolmaster whose favourite punishment was an order to write out ten verbs was considered a harsh taskmaster, but an oft-delinquent pupil is now grateful for an ineradicable knowledge of conjugations! The Key to the Exercises is also at the back of the book and there is no difficulty in taking a little peep, " just to make sure ", but the wise student will *write out* the exercise first and only then look at the correct version. It will be slower, but far, far surer in the result.

If you really get stuck, call on your nearest clergyman or minister—he has probably forgotten most of his Greek, but you will be doing him a favour if he has to stir up his memory again!

For the sake of economy no excerpts from the New Testament have been included in the book, but from Lesson XVI you will be able to start reading the simpler portions, and for this you will need a Greek Testament. The most convenient and up-to-date edition is that recently published by the British and Foreign Bible Society, which is adequate for even quite advanced study. A small dictionary will also be useful from this stage, and either *Souter's Dictionary*, published by the O.U.P., or Bagster's small dictionary, will be adequate. For further study Abbott-Smith's *Manual Lexicon of the Greek New Testament* is more comprehensive, whilst much more detailed discussion of grammar and syntax can be found in Jay's *New Testament Greek Grammar*, published by the S.P.C.K. Anything more advanced than these will lead you into the field of specialist studies.

INTRODUCTION

A lady is reported to have said to a missionary who had been engaged in translation of the New Testament into one of the Central African languages, " But why do that? If English was good enough for St. Paul, why isn't it good enough for them? " Anyone who has begun to read this book will at least not fall into that trap, but there are still many people who believe, consciously or unconsciously, that since the Bible is a sacred book the language of the Bible is in some sense " sacred language ". The fact that the Greek of the Bible is different from the Greek of Homer, Euripides, Herodotus, Thucydides and Demosthenes is obvious as soon as we begin to read it, and until a couple of generations ago there were two explanations given for this, one being that the Greek of the New Testament was a special type of language devised by the Holy Spirit for imparting Divine Truth, and the other being that it was written by non-Greeks whose own language had corrupted their Greek. Round about the turn of the century people digging in the dry sands of the Nile valley discovered masses of documents written on papyrus, a kind of material made from the dried pith of reeds, which was the most common writing-material of the ancient world. Since it is a vegetable product it is very susceptible to damp, and it is only in the bone-dry sands of Egypt that it has a chance of preservation, but it was spread over the whole of the Mediterranean at the time of the New Testament. Startling facts about these papyrus documents were that they were written in exactly the same type of Greek as the New Testament, but they were not " inspired writings ", they were letters, accounts, certificates, bills and all kinds of everyday documents, nor were they written by Jews whose Hebrew or Aramaic had " corrupted " the pure Greek of the Classical writers. The man who first made these widely known was a German scholar named Deissmann, who wrote a book called *Light from the Ancient East*, but many others have since then joined in the same work, and the results of their labours are most easily available in Moulton and Milligan's *Vocabulary of the Greek New Testament*. As a result of all these labours it was realized that the Greek of the New Testament was the common, everyday language of the first century and it is often referred to by the name " *Koine* ", which is just the Greek word for " common ".

The Gospel tells us that when Jesus was crucified an inscription was put on the Cross in Hebrew, Latin and Greek, and to people living in a country of one language like England that needs explanation (and I have seen some very strange ones produced), but I have lived for nearly twenty years in a place where all the railway stations have trilingual inscriptions on the platforms. They are in Bengali (the language of the province), Hindi (the language of the country), and English (the language most widely known by educated people). It was an everyday matter to put notices in Palestine in three languages, the language of the province (Hebrew, or more correctly, Aramaic), the official language of the Roman Empire (Latin), and the common lingua franca of the Mediterranean world (Greek), but this Greek was not the polished literary Greek of Athens which was used by authors who had a reputation for style, but the language which had been carried over the Eastern Mediterranean and as far as India, three centuries earlier, by the armies of Alexander the Great. He was not an Athenian but a Macedonian and his armies were cosmopolitan, so that the Greek they spoke was simplified and modified to be a suitable vehicle for ordinary people of many races. A serious

author considered that it was beneath his dignity to write
" Common Greek ", and for many centuries after that any
author who wanted his work to be acceptable to educated
people wrote, not in the style in which he normally spoke,
but in the style in which people spoke in Athens in the
fourth century B.C.   That is why there are no other literary
compositions in the same language as the New Testament,
and that is why until the papyri were discovered, it was
thought that this type of Greek was a peculiar " sacred
tongue ".   It was really just the opposite: the men who
wrote the New Testament were not concerned with literary
pretensions, but with getting across to as many people as
possible, in the language they could best understand, the
message which they believed was the truth for all nations.
   The language of the New Testament is " Common
Greek ", not a sacred language, as was previously thought;
but the other old idea—that the Greek has been " corrupted " by Jewish writers who were not writing their
mother-tongue—has something of truth in it.   The English
of Texas is not the same as the English of Yorkshire or
Melbourne, and all of them differ from " standard English ",
but it would be well to stand at a safe distance before telling
a Texan, or a Yorkshireman, or an Australian that his
language is " corrupt "!   Similarly, the Greek of the
people in different regions of the Mediterranean world differed, especially when it was their second language and not
their mother-tongue.   A Frenchman speaking English, or
an Englishman speaking French, tends to express himself in
the way in which he would do in his mother-tongue, and
if he is not completely conversant with the other language
he tends to appear " quaint ".   Since the mother-tongue
of almost all the New Testament writers (perhaps excluding
Luke) was some form of Semitic language, this has affected
their use of Greek.   Also, just as an Englishman writing

about a religious subject will find that his language is affected by the language of the Authorized Version, so these people also were affected by the language of their Bible, which was the Greek version of the Old Testament which we call the Septuagint. This version was translated in Alexandria for the Greek-speaking world, and since it was translated by Jews, whose mother-tongue was Hebrew, this too has been very much affected by a Hebrew style.

Another point to remember when reading the New Testament, is that all English versions are the work of a particular group, or a particular person, therefore the English style tends to be the same from Matthew to Revelation. A little acquaintance is enough to recognize whether a man is reading from the A.V., the R.V., Moffatt, or J. B. Phillips, no matter from which part of the New Testament he is reading. But the Greek of the New Testament is not so constant in style, indeed it is very varied. By the standard of literary Greek the " best " style is that of the Epistle to the Hebrews, and the next that of St. Luke, in the Third Gospel and Acts, whilst the " worst " style is that of the Book of Revelation, which is full of grammatical solecisms and is clearly written by a man who was used to speaking Hebrew, not Greek. It is clear on the grounds of style alone that the same person could not have written the Fourth Gospel and the Book of Revelation, but there must have been two different Johns.

Another point which is interesting is that the First Letter of Peter is written in quite good Greek. It is clear from the letter itself that the writer was Sylvanus (Silas), who acted as Peter's amanuensis, but it is also likely that Peter himself was able to dictate the Greek and check it. He was a Galilean, and Galilee was a bilingual area. In England it is very difficult to realize what it means to live in a bilingual or multi-lingual area, but there are some areas of the world where it is not uncommon for ordinary people to be fluent in three or four languages. Therefore it is very likely that the disciples, and Jesus himself, who were inhabitants of Galilee, would be equally at home when speaking in Greek as in Aramaic, and probably knew enough of Latin to get along with official business. There are many things in the New Testament which are more easily understood if it is realized that the events it describes and the words spoken, come from an area in which people were accustomed to speak more than one language, and in which the most common language for communication between people of different races was the language which is found in the New Testament. To misquote the lady mentioned at the beginning of this Introduction, " If Greek was good enough for Jesus and his disciples, it is good enough for us to take the trouble to learn it."

THE ALPHABET

The Letters

The heading of this chapter itself gives you a start, because the word " alphabet " comes from the name of the first two letters of the Greek alphabet—alpha and beta. Through geography you have probably also learned a third —delta—and through geometry a fourth—pi—whilst the common phrase " from alpha to omega " gives you the last. So already there are five of the twenty-four letters known to you by name, and you will probably recognize others.

Greek was originally written in capitals, and the earliest manuscripts of the New Testament are all in capitals, but later a quicker " cursive ", or running, script was devised and for the most part this superseded the former " uncial ", or capital, script. In many Greek texts printed today capital letters are only used for proper names, though some also print them at the beginning of a sentence or paragraph, but this is not necessary and you can safely leave them out at present, and pick them up as you go along. Out of the twenty-four, ten (*ABEZIKMNOT*) are exactly the same as in English, ten are completely different, and four look the same but are really different, so you should pay particular attention to these four, which are *HPYX*. Note them in the list below, and see what they stand for in Greek, so that you will not be misled.

The letters you will use are the small letters, and it is rather important to start with the correct way of writing them. If you can persuade someone to show you it is best, but if not, look carefully at the diagram, and, in particular, start writing each letter at the point indicated by the asterisk. Nearly all the letters can be written without lifting the pen from the paper, and this is how they should be made. They should not be joined together, but should each be separate, just like English when it is " printed " by hand. Notice that $\beta\delta\zeta\theta\lambda\xi\varphi\psi$ protrude above the top line, and $\beta\gamma\zeta\eta\mu\varrho\varsigma\varphi\chi\psi$ below the bottom line. The tails of $\zeta\xi\varsigma$ should be quite short, but definitely below the line, and the bottoms of ν and υ should be carefully distinguished, as also the small tangent at the top of σ which distinguishes it from o.

Letter	English	Greek small	Capital
Alpha	a	α	A
Beta	b	β	B
Gamma	g	γ	Γ
Delta	d	δ	Δ
Epsilon	e (short)	ε	E
Zeta	z	ζ	Z
Eta	e (long)	η	H
Theta	th	θ	Θ
Iota	i	ι	I
Kappa	k	$\varkappa$	K
La(m)bda	l	λ	Λ

Letter	English	Greek small	Capital
Mu	m	μ	M
Nu	n	ν	N
Xi	x	ξ	Ξ
Omikron	o (short)	o	O
Pi	p	π	Π
Rho	rh	ϱ	P
Sigma	s	σ or ς	Σ
Tau	t	τ	T
Upsilon	u	υ	Y
Phi	ph	φ	Φ
Chi	ch	χ	X
Psi	ps	ψ	Ψ
Omega	o (long)	ω	ω or Ω

Notes on Letters

Greek has two extra vowels compared with English, since there are two pairs (ε–η and o–ω) of which the former is the short form and the latter the long form of the same sound. The letter ι is never dotted in Greek, and sometimes it is written underneath another letter, as mentioned in the next lesson.

Two consonants should be noted particularly:

1. Sigma has two forms—ς, which is found *only* at the end of a word, and σ, which is found at *any other position* than last letter. E.g. the word for " resurrection " in Greek is anastasis, which is written ἀναστασις.

2. Gamma takes the place of a nasal sound (n) before the guttural letters γκξχ, so that the combinations are pronounced as follows: γγ—ng, γκ—nk, γξ—nx, γχ—nch. If two words are combined, and one originally ends with a ν and the other starts with a guttural,

the first is modified according to this rule, e.g.
συν + γενης = συγγενης.

Pronunciation

Apart from this one peculiarity Greek pronunciation is straightforward, since letters are always pronounced the same, and all letters are pronounced. There has been much argument about the way the ancient Greeks themselves pronounced the language, but in general there are two accepted ways of pronouncing Classical and New Testament Greek (neither of which is the way in which Modern Greek is pronounced!). Since your main concern is not to speak the language, but to read the New Testament, it does not really matter which way you use, but here is the Revised Pronunciation decided on by the Classical Association some years ago, which is the one most commonly used.

α— (i) long as in father
　　(ii) short as in cat
β—as in bad
γ—as in go (never soft as in gentle)
δ—as in did
ε—as in get
ζ—as " dz " in adze
η—a pure vowel not found in standard English; like a Yorkshireman's " eh " or French père
θ—soft as in thin
ι— (i) long as in feet
　　(ii) short as in fit
κ—as in king
λ—as in long
μ—as in man

ν—as in not
ξ—as in wax
ο—as in got
π—as in poor
ρ—as in rich
σς—as in mouse
τ—as in tea
υ—a thin vowel like French u
　　(i) long as in rue
　　(ii) short as in du
φ—as English f in fish
χ—as Scots ch in loch (never as ch in church)
ψ—as in lapse
ω—a pure long vowel not found in standard English; like a Yorkshireman's " oh "

Diphthongs

αι—as in Is*ai*ah   αυ—as in g*ow*n
ει—as in gr*ey*   ευ, ηυ—as in f*ew*
οι—as in b*oi*l   ου—as in m*oo*n
υι—as in French l*ui*, almost like English *wee*

Now look at some of the things around you and try to
write down and pronounce their names: You are probably
sitting on a καθεδρα by the side of a τραπεζα and you are
reading a βιβλιον which you are holding in your χειρ.
You are writing with a καλαμος which you probably hold
in your δεξια χειρ, though some people use the αριστερα
χειρ. You are studying Greek, so you are a μαθητης,
and using this book you can be your own διδασκαλος. If
someone asks what you are doing with the καλαμος you
can say, " γραφω ". I hope the lesson has not been so
indigestible that you are suffering from δυσπεψια.

KEY

(cover this up until you have done the exercise)

You should have been able to guess the meaning of the
Greek words in the above paragraph, but here you can
check them with the pronunciation.

καθεδρα—kathedra—chair, seat—a cathedral is a Bishop's
seat.

τραπεζα—trapedza—table—but probably not trapezium-
shaped!

βιβλιον—biblion—book—hence Bible and bibliography.

χειρ—cheir—hand—hence a *chir*opodist, who treats hands
and feet.

καλαμος—kalamos—pen—originally a reed, for writing on
wax.

δεξια χειρ—dexia cheir—right hand—the connected word in Latin gives us ambi*dex*trous.

ἀριστερα χειρ—aristera cheir—left hand.

μαθητης—mathētēs—a learner, student—nowadays the word is monopolized by the *mathe*maticians, but originally included all studies.

διδασκαλος—didaskalos—teacher—hence didactic.

γραφω—graphō—I am writing—hence graph and all the words which end in -graphy.

δυσπεψια—dyspepsia, since the Greek υ has come into its English derivatives as " y ", almost without exception.

This set of words contains all the letters of the Greek alphabet, so write them out several times until you can do it fluently.

LESSON II

BREATHINGS, IOTA SUBSCRIPT, READING

Check the list of words you have learned to read, and add another—ἱματιον, pronounced " himation ", meaning a garment. Perhaps you wondered why ἀριστερα was written with a comma over the first letter, and now you see that ἱματιον also has a comma, but it is turned the other way round. The first comma makes no difference to the pronunciation of ἀριστερα, but the second one adds an aspirate to ἱματιον. In Greek there is no letter " h ", but there are words beginning with an aspirate, which is indicated in this way. These two commas are called " breathings ", and the first one (᾿) is a *smooth* breathing, which does not affect the pronunciation of the letter, whilst the second (῾) is a *rough* breathing, which gives it an aspirate.

There are five simple rules about breathings:

1. Every word in Greek which begins with a vowel has a breathing.
2. If the word is aspirated it has a ROUGH breathing (῾), if it is unaspirated it has a SMOOTH breathing (᾿); IT MUST HAVE ONE OR OTHER, IF IT BEGINS WITH A VOWEL.
3. If it begins with a diphthong (two vowels pronounced together), the breathing is put on the second vowel.
4. Capitals have the breathing just in front of the top of the letters, e.g. ᾿Αδαμ, ᾿Ιησους, ῾Εβραιοι, ᾿Ισαακ, ῾Ιερουσαλημ.
5. The letter ῥ beginning a word is usually given a breathing, and that is why words in English derived from Greek are spelt " rh ", like rhythm, rhombus, rhubarb, and rhinoceros.

7

Now look at these sentences:

ὁ διδασκαλος ἐστιν ἐπι τῃ καθεδρᾳ—The teacher is on the chair.

το βιβλιον ἐστιν ἐπι τῃ τραπεζῃ—The book is on the table.

το ἱματιον ἐστιν ἐπι τῳ διδασκαλῳ—The garment is on the teacher.

The long vowels α, η, ω when combined with ι take "iota subscript" (written under). These are mostly, but not always, at the end of words.

Punctuation

The following signs of punctuation are used in printed Greek, though it must be remembered the early manuscripts of the New Testament did not have any punctuation at all.

, comma　　　· semi-colon　　　. full-stop　　　; question-mark

Notice particularly the semi-colon and question-mark which are different from English usage.

Accents

Printed Greek also has accents on words, ' ´ ¯, but these were invented by a grammarian in the third century B.C. to help people read the poetry of Homer. They do not appear in manuscripts before the seventh century A.D., so if people managed to read the New Testament without them for five or six hundred years, we can probably do the same. In a few cases they distinguish words which have different meanings, but the differences can usually be inferred from the context. In some cases they are completely arbitrary, and the present writer confesses that after thirty years he is still shaky on accents!

Here is the Lord's Prayer in Greek. First cover up the key and then try to read it through. Read it again before each lesson and you will soon have it by heart.

Πατερ ἡμων ὁ ἐν τοις οὐρανοις, ἁγιασθητω το ὀνομα σου. ἐλθετω ἡ βασιλεια σου. γενηθητω το θελημα σου, ὡς ἐν οὐρανῳ και ἐπι γης. τον ἀρτον ἡμων τον ἐπιουσιον δος ἡμιν σημερον. και ἀφες ἡμιν τα ὀφειληματα ἡμων ὡς και ἡμεις ἀφηκαμεν τοις ὀφειλεταις ἡμων, και μη εἰσενεγκῃς ἡμας εἰς πειρασμον, ἀλλα ῥυσαι ἡμας ἀπο του πονηρου. ὁτι σου ἐστιν ἡ βασιλεια και ἡ δυναμις και ἡ δοξα εἰς τους αἰωνας. ἀμην.

KEY

Pater hēmōn ho en tois ooranois, hagiasthētō to onoma soo.   elthetō hē basileia soo.   genēthētō to thelēma soo, hōs en ooranō kai epi gēs.   ton arton hēmōn ton epioosion dos hēmin sēmeron.   kai aphes hēmin ta opheilēmata hēmōn hōs kai hēmeis aphēkamen tois opheiletais hēmōn. kai mē eisenenkēs hēmas eis peirasmon, alla rhoosai hēmas apo too ponēroo.   hoti soo estin hē basileia kai hē dunamis kai hē doxa eis toos aiōnas. amēn.

READING PRACTICE

Check the words you learned in Lessons I and II.

διδασκαλος, μαθητης, τραπεζα, καθεδρα, βιβλιον, χειρ, ἱματιον.

Now, how many Greek words do you know? Nine or ten? You have learnt nine or ten in these two lessons, but what about all the words that you knew before? Here are fifty of them, some which you will find in the New Testament, some from other Greek, but all of which have come into English, and other languages, almost unchanged. Write them in English and you will see the meanings.

Nos. 1–24 are mostly classical, nos. 25–50 are all New Testament.

1. ὀρχηστρα	18. συνοψις	35. στιγμα
2. ἰδεα	19. θεσις	36. χαρακτηρ
3. κινημα	20. διλημμα	37. σκηνη
4. δραμα	21. δευτερονομος	38. παθος
5. κλιμαξ	22. παραλυσις	39. μιασμα
6. κωμα	23. τηλεφωνη	40. ἀντιθεσις
7. ἠχω	24. βακτηρια	41. βαθος
8. νεμεσις	25. διαγνωσις	42. αὐτοματον
9. ἐμφασις	26. ἀναλυσις	43. δογμα
10. ὑποθεσις	27. γενεσις	44. ἠθος
11. πνευμονια	28. ψυχη	45. κοσμος
12. ἀσθμα	29. δυσεντερια	46. κανων
13. φθισις	30. ζωνη	47. θερμος
14. χαος	31. ἀσβεστος	48. βασις
15. διπλωμα	32. κρισις	49. χορος
16. ἀτλας	33. καταστροφη	50. ἐξοδος
17. κρατηρ	34. ἀναθεμα	

Notes on the Greek words

Generally in transliteration " y " replaces " v ", and " c " replaces " κ ". 1 Originally the place where the chorus dance in the theatre; 3 from a root which means " move "; 4 root δρα- " do "; 5 orig. " ladder "; 6 root φα- " speak "; 10 lit. place under ; 11 root πνε- " blow " or " breathe " (cf. pneumatic tyres); 13 root φθι- " deteriorate "; 15 orig. something doubled-up; 16 the name of the giant who held up the sky, from root meaning " untiring "; 17 lit. " mixing-bowl ", and therefore the bowl-shaped top of a volcano; 18 lit. " seeing-together ", root ὀπ- " seeing ", hence " optical " etc.; 19 lit. " placing "; 20 lit. " double-taking "; 21 lit. " second law "; 22 lit. " loosening " of control of limbs; 23, 24 are modern Greek words, 23 is from the roots τηλε- " far " and φωνε- " speak ", 24 is lit. " little rods " from the shape of microbes; 25 root γνω- " know "; 26 lit. " loosening-up "; 27 root γεν- " become "; 29 lit. " bad-inside "; 30 lit. " belt "; 31 roots α- " not " and σβε- " extinguish "; 32 lit. " judging "; 33 root στρεφ- " turn "; 37 orig. tent for actors' dressing-room, which was decorated for a backcloth; 40 lit. " placing against "; 42 root αὐτο- " self "; 43. lit. " that which is decided "; 46 lit. " rule ", also used of a carpenter's measure; 50 roots ἐξ " out " and ὁδος " way ".

Now turn to Matthew v. 1-16 in your Greek New Testament. Don't bother to try to make out the meaning, but just read the words, and you will find that soon several of them will be obvious. Then, if you want more practice, turn to some other passage which you know well, and read it through in Greek, noticing how some of the meanings become clear as you read.

Try to spot English words, and look them up in the English Dictionary, to see whether they come from Greek or not.

DECLENSIONS OF NOUNS AND ADJECTIVES

1. ἀγαθη κορη βλεπει κακον ἀνθρωπον.
   A good girl sees a bad man.
2. ὠ ἀγαθη κορη, τηρει.
   O good girl, watch out.
3. ὁ κακος ἀνθρωπος ἁρπαζει την ἀγαθην κορην.
   The bad man seizes the good girl.
4. " ὠ κακε ἀνθρωπε " λεγει ἡ κορη τῳ κακῳ ἀνθρωπῳ,
   " ἀπελθε ".
   " O bad man ", says the good girl to the bad man,
   " go away ".
5. ὁ κακος ἀνθρωπος κλεπτει την της ἀγαθης κορης πηραν.
   The bad man steals the good girl's bag.
6. και λεγει τῃ ἀγαθη κορη κακον λογον.
   And says to the good girl a bad word.
7. ἡ ἀγαθη κορη τυπτει το του κακου ἀνθρωπου προσωπον.
   The good girl smacks the bad man's face.

Let us look at the persons involved in this episode and
see what happens to them. When we look at the good
girl we see that in English she is the same all through,
except that she gets " 's " in sentence 5, but in Greek she
changes quite a lot. These changes are quite familiar to
Indian students whose languages treat words in the same
way. The alteration in the endings of words to show their
different function in the sentence is called INFLECTION, and
Greek, like most Indian languages (but unlike English), is
inflected.

Let us look, then, at the function of the girl in each sentence.

In sentence 1 she is the DOER of the action;

12

In sentence 2 she is the PERSON ADDRESSED;
In sentence 3 she is the OBJECT of the action;
In sentence 5 she is the POSSESSOR of the bag;
In sentence 6 she is the INDIRECT OBJECT. The direct object is the word, and she is the person to whom it is said, and who is therefore indirectly affected by the action.

Let us now look at the function of the man, and see how he also changes.

In sentence 1 he is the OBJECT of her action;
In sentence 3 he is the DOER of the action;
In sentence 4 he is the PERSON ADDRESSED;
In sentence 4 also he is the PERSON INDIRECTLY AFFECTED;
In sentence 7 he is the POSSESSOR of the face.

There are three points to notice:

1. both the girl and the man change their endings, but
2. they do not have the same set of endings, and
3. " good " and " bad " also change *their* endings, and also the endings of the girl's adjectives are different from the endings of the man's.

The name for the part of the word which does not change (ἀγαθ-, κορ-, κακ-, ἀνθρωπ-) is the STEM, and the name for the part which changes is the ENDING, whilst the different forms of the words are called different CASES. In Greek there are FIVE CASES:

NOMINATIVE case, expressing the DOER (Lat.—nomen— name).
VOCATIVE case, expressing PERSON ADDRESSED (Lat.— voco—call).
ACCUSATIVE case, expressing the OBJECT.

GENITIVE case, expressing POSSESSOR or ORIGIN (cf. Genesis).

DATIVE case, expressing INDIRECT OBJECT (Lat.—do— give).

In the examples above there is ONE girl and ONE man, and all the cases are in the SINGULAR NUMBER, but there are other endings to express the PLURAL NUMBER. (In Classical Greek there is also a dual number, but you are spared that.)

The different sets of endings are accounted for because the man is MASCULINE GENDER and the girl is FEMININE GENDER.

Now it is clear that since the *form* of the word decides its particular function, it does not matter what is its position in the sentence, since it would have the same meaning in any of the following orders:

ἀγαθη κορη βλεπει κακον ἀνθρωπον
κακον ἀνθρωπον βλεπει ἀγαθη κορη
βλεπει κακον ἀνθρωπον ἀγαθη κορη
ἀγαθη κορη κακον ἀνθρωπον βλεπει

However, it is usually true that the order in the New Testament is Subject—Verb—Object, and if the order is varied it is done to lay emphasis on a particular word, by putting it in a prominent position, either as first word, or as last word, in the sentence.

It is also most important to notice that adjectives must have the same function as the noun to which they refer, and must, therefore, be in the same CASE; they must also have the same NUMBER, and the same GENDER. A singular noun must have a singular adjective, a plural noun must have a plural adjective; a masculine noun must have a masculine adjective, and so on.

(*Note:* GENDER in Greek is not the same as SEX. Males

are usually masculine and females feminine, though κορασιον, "a young girl", is neuter; but things may be of any gender, e.g. "table" and "chair" are feminine, "house" is masculine, and "book" is neuter. The gender is seen from the *form* of the word.)

We can now look at the forms of the words we have met already.

The forms ending in -η are called FIRST DECLENSION, the forms ending in -ος are called SECOND DECLENSION, and since adjectives have both forms we can get everything together by taking an adjective as an example.

κακος—bad

	Masc.	*Singular* *Fem.*	*Neut.*
Nom.	κακ-ος	κακ-η	κακ-ον
Voc.	κακ-ε	κακ-η	κακ-ον
Acc.	κακ-ον	κακ-ην	κακ-ον
Gen.	κακ-ου	κακ-ης	κακ-ου
Dat.	κακ-ῳ	κακ-ῃ	κακ-ῳ

	Masc.	*Plural* *Fem.*	*Neut.*
Nom.	κακ-οι	κακ-αι	κακ-α
Voc.	κακ-οι	κακ-αι	κακ-α
Acc.	κακ-ους	κακ-ας	κακ-α
Gen.	κακ-ων	κακ-ων	κακ-ων
Dat.	κακ-οις	κακ-αις	κακ-οις

ἀγαθος has exactly the same endings.
ἀνθρωπος has the endings of the first column.
κορη has the endings of the second column.

Note: In all neuter nouns and adjectives the nom., voc. and acc. are the same, and all neuter plurals have alpha.

The dative case always has an iota, and the genitive plural always has -ων.

Sometimes the plural of an adjective may be used to express a general class, in which case the gender of the adjective is expressed in English by adding a word like " men " or " women " or " things ", e.g. κακοι may mean " bad men ", κακαι " bad women " and κακα " evil things ".

THERE IS NO WORD IN GREEK TO EXPRESS " THINGS " IN A GENERAL SENSE.   THIS IS ALWAYS DONE BY USING A NEUTER FORM OF AN ADJECTIVE OR THE NEUTER ARTICLE.

EXERCISE Ia

1. ὁ ἀνθρωπος ἐστιν* ἀγαθος.
2. ὁ ἀγαθος διδασκαλος γραφει τους λογους.
3. ἡ κορη βλεπει το του κακου ἀνθρωπου προσωπον.†
4. ὁ ἀδελφος ἁρπαζει το του δουλου ἱματιον.
5. ὁ θεος τηρει τον κοσμον.
6. ὁ λογος της γραφης ἐστιν ἀγαθος.
7. το βιβλιον ἐστιν ἐν τη πηρα.
8. ὁ ἀνθρωπος καθιζει ἐπι τη καθεδρᾳ.

EXERCISE Ib

1. The girl is good.
2. The bad man sees the good girl.
3. The teacher's book is good.
4. The girl speaks a word to the brother.
5. O man, God is good.

Vocabulary I

Nouns

ἀνθρωπος —man
ἀδελφος— brother
διδασκαλος—teacher
δουλος—servant
θεος—god
κοσμος—world
λογος—word

κορη—girl
πηρα—bag
καθεδρα—seat
γραφη—writing
ἱματιον—garment
προσωπον—face
βιβλιον—book

Adjectives

ἀγαθος—good
κακος—bad
σοφος—wise
πρωτος—first

καλος—beautiful
ἐσχατος—last
πιστος—faithful
τριτος—third

Verbs

ἐστι(ν)—is
γραφει—writes
βλεπει—sees
ἁρπαζει—snatches
ἐν—in

τηρει—watches, keeps
καθιζει—sits
διδασκει—teaches
λεγει—says

(*Note:* * When ἐστι is followed by a vowel it adds a ν to help the pronunciation.

† The possessive genitive is usually placed between the article and noun of the thing possessed.)

EXERCISE II

Write down the English words which are derived from the following Greek words:

νεος—λογος   μεσος—ποταμος   φιλος—ἀδελφος
οἰκος—νομος   θρονος   ἀριστος—κρατος
τυραννος   θεος—λογος   χλωρος—φυλλον
δημος—κρατος   μακρος—κοσμος   μικρος—σκοπος
κρυπτος—γραφη   ὁμοιος—παθος   ἀνεμος—μετρον
ἀγγελος   ζῳον—λογος   βιος—λογος
εἰδωλον   ὀρθος—δοξα   μικρος—φωνη
ὑμνος   φιλος—σοφια   κυκλος
ἱερος—ἀρχη   αὐτος—γραφη   μεγας—φωνη
μονος—ἀρχη   παλαιος—γραφη

The following are the literal meanings of the words in English:

new—word	middle—river	friend—brother
house—law	—	best—rule
autocratic ruler	god—word	green—leaf
people—rule	large—world	small—looking
hidden—writing	like—suffering	wind—measure
messenger	animal—word	life—word
shadow, image	straight—opinion	little—sound
—	friend—wisdom	circle
sacred—rule	self—writing	big—sound
alone—rule	old—writing	

LESSON V

THE DEFINITE ARTICLE

Greek has no word for " a " (indefinite article) but it has a word for " the " (definite article).

It is used as in English, AND ALSO

(i) With Abstract Nouns, e.g. Wisdom—ἡ σοφια.
(ii) With words which signify whole classes, e.g. Men are good—οἱ ἀνθρωποι εἰσιν ἀγαθοι.
(iii) With Proper Nouns, e.g. Jesus—ὁ Ἰησους (but this is sometimes disregarded in the New Testament).

The declension of the article is as follows:

	Singular			*Plural*		
	Masc.	Fem.	Neut.	Masc.	Fem.	Neut.
Nom.	ὁ	ἡ	το	οἱ	αἱ	τα
Acc.	τον	την	το	τους	τας	τα
Gen.	του	της	του	των	των	των
Dat.	τῳ	τῃ	τῳ	τοις	ταις	τοις

Try to translate the following sentences from Greek authors:

1. μεγα βιβλιον μεγα κακον (Callimachus).
2. ὁ ἀνεξεταστος (unexamined) βιος οὐ βιωτος ἀνθρωπῳ (Plato).
3. ἀνθρωπος πολιτικον ζῳον (Aristotle).
4. ὁ φιλος ἐστιν ἀλλος (other) αὐτος.
5. χρονος παιδευει τους σοφους. (παιδευει educates).
6. ἐν ἀρχῃ ἠν ὁ λογος και ὁ λογος ἠν προς (towards) τον θεον και θεος ἠν ὁ λογος.
7. ἐγω εἰμι το Ἀλφα και το Ὠμεγα, ἀρχη και τελος, ὁ πρωτος και ὁ ἐσχατος.

19

The Verb " to be "

The verb " to be " does not express action, but tells us something about the state, condition or character of the subject, e.g. The man *is* bad; John *is* a doctor; Mary *was* in the house. " Bad " and " doctor " are not objects, since they are not affected by any action and therefore they are not put into the accusative case in Greek. They *complete* the sense of the sentence, so they are *complements*, they *predicate* some quality of the subject, so they are *predicates*.

RULE: THE VERB " TO BE " TAKES THE SAME CASE AFTER IT AS BEFORE IT.

The Indicative tenses of the verb " to be " are as follows:

Present	*Past*	*Future*
Singular		
I am—$\varepsilon i\mu\iota$	I was—$\mathring{\eta}\mu\eta\nu$	I shall be—$\mathring{\varepsilon}\sigma o\mu a\iota$
You are—εi	You were— $\mathring{\eta}\sigma\theta a, \mathring{\eta}\varsigma$	You will be—$\mathring{\varepsilon}\sigma\varepsilon\iota$
He is She is $\Big\}$—$\mathring{\varepsilon}\sigma\tau\iota(\nu)$ It is	He was She was $\Big\}$—$\mathring{\eta}\nu$ It was	He will be She will be $\Big\}$—$\mathring{\varepsilon}\sigma\tau a\iota$ It will be
Plural		
We are—$\mathring{\varepsilon}\sigma\mu\varepsilon\nu$	We were—$\mathring{\eta}\mu\varepsilon\nu$	We shall be— $\mathring{\varepsilon}\sigma o\mu\varepsilon\theta a$
You are—$\mathring{\varepsilon}\sigma\tau\varepsilon$	You were—$\mathring{\eta}\tau\varepsilon$	You will be—$\mathring{\varepsilon}\sigma\varepsilon\sigma\theta\varepsilon$
They are—$\varepsilon i\sigma\iota(\nu)$	They were—$\mathring{\eta}\sigma a\nu$	They will be— $\mathring{\varepsilon}\sigma o\nu\tau a\iota$

(*Note:* In English " you " may be singular or plural; in turning it into Greek the context must be carefully noted to see which it is, and the proper form used.)

NOUNS IN -o—SECOND DECLENSION

It may seem a little strange to consider the Second Declension Nouns before we consider the First Declension, but since we have already looked at the Adjectives, it is convenient to start with the first column, and to recognize the superiority of the masculine!

The prevailing vowel in the endings of this declension is -o and words ending in -ος in the nominative are all masculine, except about half-a-dozen, which are feminine, whilst words ending in -ον in the nominative are all neuter. These latter have -α in the nominative, vocative and accusative plural.

| | Masculine | | Neuter | |
	Singular	Plural	Singular	Plural
Nom.	λογος	λογοι	βιβλιον	βιβλια
Voc.	λογε	λογοι	βιβλιον	βιβλια
Acc.	λογον	λογους	βιβλιον	βιβλια
Gen.	λογου	λογων	βιβλιου	βιβλιων
Dat.	λογῳ	λογοις	βιβλιῳ	βιβλιοις

Here are some more with their meanings:

ἀποστολος—apostle
ἀρτος—bread
θανατος—death
κυριος—lord
λαος—people

ἀργυριον—silver, money
δαιμονιον—demon
δενδρον—tree
ἐργον—work
εὐαγγελιον—gospel
ἱερον—temple
παιδιον—child
πλοιον—boat

And these three are FEMININE:

ἐρημος—desert
παρθενος—maiden, girl
ὁδος—way, road

προβατον—sheep
τεκνον—child
σαββατον—sabbath
σημειον—sign, miracle

EXERCISE IIIa

1. το δενδρον ἐστιν ἀγαθον.
2. ὁ θεος φιλει τους ἀγαθους.
3. τα παιδια ἠν ἐν τῳ ποταμῳ.
4. ὁ φοβος του κυριου ἐστιν ἀρχη της σοφιας.
5. ὁ λαος οὐ τηρει τον λογον του θεου.

EXERCISE IIIb

6. The demons are in the world.
7. The apostle sees the books of the children.
8. The life of men is good.
9. Death is the lord of men.
10. The child is in the boat.

Vocabulary

φιλει—loves
οὐ—not (put immediately BEFORE the word it qualifies)
φοβος—fear

χρυσος—gold
ἐν—in

(*Note:* Neuter plural nouns are often followed by a singular verb, as in sentence 3.)

LESSON VII

NOUNS IN -α AND -η—FIRST DECLENSION

There are four types of nouns in the First Declension, the first three being all Feminine and the fourth being Masculine.

1. Nouns ending in -η declined like the feminine of κακος.

	Singular	Plural
Nom.	κορη	κοραι
Voc.	κορη	κοραι
Acc.	κορην	κορας
Gen.	κορης	κορων
Dat.	κορη	κοραις

You have already had:

ἀρχη—beginning	διαθηκη—testament
σκηνη—tent	ζωη—life
γραφη—writing	ζωνη—belt
καταστροφη—catastrophe	φωνη—sound, voice

Here are some more:

ἀγαπη—love	συναγωγη—synagogue
γη—earth	τεχνη—art, skill
λυπη—grief	εἰρηνη—peace
ὀργη—anger	κεφαλη—head
ἐντολη—commandment	παραβολη—parable
δικαιοσυνη—righteousness	ψυχη—soul, life

2. Nouns whose stems end in ε, ι or ϱ have -α instead of -η in all their endings. These are called "α-pure" words.

23

	Singular	*Plural*
Nom.	πηρα	πηραι
Voc.	πηρα	πηραι
Acc.	πηραν	πηρας
Gen.	πηρας	πηρων
Dat.	πηρᾳ	πηραις

Note: κορη is an exception to this rule, but it is not found in the New Testament and it has served our purpose, so can now be ignored.

You have already had:

σοφια—wisdom   δυσεντερια—dysentery
καθεδρα—seat

Here are some more:

χωρα—country   ἐπαγγελια—promise
θυρα—door   ἐξουσια—authority
ἡμερα—day   παραγγελια—commandment
καρδια—heart   βασιλεια—kingdom
ὡρα—hour   ἁμαρτια—sin
γενεα—generation   ἀληθεια—truth
ἐκκλησια—assembly   χαρα—joy

3. Nouns with -α in the Nominative, and stems NOT ending in ε, ι or ρ have -ης, -ῃ in Genitive and Dative singular. These are called " α-impure ".

The only ones you are likely to meet are:

γλωσσα—tongue   δοξα—opinion, glory
θαλασσα—sea   τραπεζα—table

Note also: Adjectives with stems ending in ε, ι or ρ also have α-pure endings, like:

	Singular		
	Masc.	*Fem.*	*Neut.*
Nom.	μιχρος	μιχρα	μιχρον
Voc.	μιχρε	μιχρα	μιχρον
Acc.	μιχρον	μιχραν	μιχρον
Gen.	μιχρου	μιχρας	μιχρου
Dat.	μιχρω	μιχρα	μιχρω

	Plural		
	Masc.	*Fem.*	*Neut.*
Nom.	μιχροι	μιχραι	μιχρα
Voc.	μιχροι	μιχραι	μιχρα
Acc.	μιχρους	μιχρας	μιχρα
Gen.	μιχρων	μιχρων	μιχρων
Dat.	μιχροις	μιχραις	μιχροις

Like this are:

ἱερος—sacred	δευτερος—second	ἀξιος—worthy
ἁγιος—holy	δικαιος—just	ἑτερος—other
ἰδιος—own	καθαρος—pure	πονηρος—wicked
ὁμοιος—like	παλαιος—ancient	νεος—new

4. The first three classes are all Feminine, and the fourth class is Masculine. These nouns all indicate a profession or permanent characteristic of a man, and all except one end in -της. (The parallel Latin ending, from which many English words are derived, is -tor, e.g. doctor, actor, prosecutor, rector, etc.)

	Singular	*Plural*
Nom.	μαθητης	μαθηται
Voc.	μαθητα	μαθηται
Acc.	μαθητην	μαθητας
Gen.	μαθητου	μαθητων
Dat.	μαθητη	μαθηταις

Like this are:

βαπτιστης—Baptist   δεσποτης—master
κλεπτης—thief   τελωνης—tax-collector
προφητης—prophet   ὑποκριτης—play-actor, hypocrite
στρατιωτης—soldier   κριτης—judge
πολιτης—citizen   λῃστης—robber
ἐργατης—workman

Also Proper Nouns like ᾿Ιωαννης, ᾿Ιορδανης, ῾Ηρωδης.

(*Note:* (i) To show that they are masculine, and to make it different from the nominative, the genitive is in -ου.

(ii) In the vocative they have -α.

(iii) One common noun, and a few Proper Nouns have -α for η: a young man—νεανιας—has singular νεανιας, νεανια, νεανιαν, νεανιου, νεανιᾳ.)

EXERCISE IVa

1. ἡ γλωσσα πολλων (many) ἐστιν αἰτια κακων.
2. ὁ βιος βραχυς (short) ἡ τεχνη μακρα (Hippocrates).
3. λυπης ἰατρος ἐστιν ὁ χρηστος φιλος (Menander).
4. ὁ θεος ἀγαπη ἐστιν, και ὁ μενων (he who remains) ἐν τῃ ἀγαπῃ μενει ἐν τῳ θεῳ και ὁ θεος ἐν αὐτῳ (him).
5. ἡ δικαιοσυνη και ἡ ἀληθεια και ἡ ἀγαπη εἰσιν ἐν τῃ βασιλειᾳ του θεου.

EXERCISE IVb

6. The peace of God watches over the souls on earth.
7. God sees the grief of men's hearts and saves them (αὐτους).
8. The world is in sin and does not have love.
9. The apostle writes the Scriptures.
10. The voice of the Lord speaks words of truth.

αἰτια—cause
βιος—life
και—and
ἐν—in, on (followed by Dative) (see Lesson XXII)
ἰατρος—doctor
μακρος—long
χρηστος—good, kind

οὐ, οὐκ, οὐχ—not (see note below)
γραφαι—Scriptures
μενει—remains
σωζει—saves
ἐχει—has
λαλει—speaks

(*Note:* The first negative is used before a word beginning with a consonant, the second before a word beginning with a smooth breathing, and the third before a word beginning with a rough breathing.)

EXERCISE Va
(Some New Testament verses)

1. ἀγαπητοι, οὐκ ἐντολην καινην γραφω, ἀλλ᾽ ἐντολην παλαιαν.
2. ἡ ἐντολη ἡ παλαια ἐστιν ὁ λογος ὁν (which) ἠκουσατε (you heard).
3. παιδια, ἐσχατη ὡρα ἐστιν.
4. ἐν τουτῳ (in this) φανερα (clear) ἐστι τα τεκνα του θεου και τα τεκνα του διαβολου.
5. ἡ ἐντολη αὐτου (his) ζωη αἰωνιος ἐστιν.
6. οὐκ ἐστι παρα (from) θεου ὁ ἀνθρωπος, ὁτι (because) το σαββατον οὐ τηρει.
7. ἐγω εἰμι ἡ ὁδος και ἡ ἀληθεια και ἡ ζωη.
8. πολλοι (many) ἐσονται πρωτοι ἐσχατοι και οἱ ἐσχατοι πρωτοι.
9. το τελος (end) της παραγγελιας ἐστιν ἀγαπη ἐκ καθαρας καρδιας.
10. κατεπαυσεν (rested) ὁ θεος ἐν τῃ ἡμερᾳ τῃ ἑβδομῃ ἀπο (from) παντων των ἐργων αὐτου.

(*Note:* αἰώνιος—eternal—has the same form in feminine as masculine (see Lesson XX). ἀπο, παρα—from (see Lesson XXII).)

EXERCISE Vb

Write down the Greek equivalents, in the proper cases, of the words in italics:

The life of a robber is not always happy. No one offers him *love*, he receives no *glory*, and *in his heart* he knows *the grief* of loneliness. But *he has skill* and cunning *in his work*. One day *a robber* saw a *tax-collector* going along the road. *The man* carried *a bag* and *in the bag* was *gold*. *The robber* waited until *the other man* came near and called to him. *The tax-collector* turned *his head* and saw *the robber* but did not know what to do. The robber asked him how he got *the gold* and the tax-collector showed him a *sheet of paper* on which was written *the law* of income-tax. The robber said, " Your *skill* in robbery is better than mine; keep your *gold, Master*."

(Sheet of paper—χαρτης.)

LESSON VIII

THE VERB—PRESENT TENSE

Verbs alter their endings to denote:
 (i) The person who does the action (e.g. I write, he writes).
 (ii) The time at which it is done (e.g. I write, I wr*ote*).

In English these variations only apply to a few parts of the verb, but in Indian languages and in Greek they apply to all. In Greek there are six different endings in each tense, three in the singular, called first, second, and third persons, and three in the plural (1s.—I, 2s.—you, 3s.—he, she, it; 1p.—we, 2p.—you, 3p.—they).

In English the different tenses (Past, Present, Future) are usually expressed by using an auxiliary verb, parts of the verbs " to be " and " to have ", but in Greek this is also done by altering the endings. This means that in Greek the form of the verb indicates not only the action, but the person doing it and the time. γραφω means " I write " or " I am writing ", and it is not necessary to use ἐγω before it because the ending -ω indicates the person.

The endings of the Present Indicative Tense in Greek are:

Singular	*Plural*
1st person I—ω	We—ομεν
2nd person You—εις	You—ετε
3rd person He, she, it—ει	They—ουσι

You have already met some verbs in the third person singular, γραφει, βλεπει, ἁρπαζει, καθιζει, μενει, σωζει, ἐχει.

As with the nouns, the part of the verb which is constant

29

is called the STEM, and the part which changes is called the ENDING. If you remove the third person singular ending (-ει) from the above verbs you can add the other endings and get the complete Present Tense. To repeat all the forms of a tense is called "TO CONJUGATE". Here is the conjugation of the Present Tense of γραφω.

	Singular	Plural
1st person	γραφω	γραφομεν
2nd person	γραφεις	γραφετε
3rd person	γραφει	γραφουσι(ν)

(*Note:* The third person plural, like ἐστι, adds -ν before a following vowel to help pronunciation.)

A verb is usually referred to, and listed in dictionaries, by the first person singular of the present tense.

Here are some more verbs:

ἀκουω—hear ἀποθνησκω—die ἀποστελλω—send
βαλλω—throw ἐγειρω—rouse ἐσθιω—eat
εὑρισκω—find κρινω—judge λαμβανω—
λεγω—say πιστευω—believe   take, receive
γινωσκω—know μανθανω—learn πινω—drink
κλεπτω—steal ἀγω—lead κατακρινω—condemn
χαιρω—rejoice λυω—loosen διδασκω—teach

ὁτε—when κριτης—judge ψευστης—liar
ὁτι—that, because νεκρος—dead σωτηρια—salvation
ἀλλα—but εἰ—if

EXERCISE VI

ὁτε ἀνθρωπος λεγει ὁτι ἐστιν ἀγαθος, γινωσκω ὁτι ψευστης ἐστι. ἐν ἀνθρωποις ἡ ἁμαρτια μενει και οὐχ εὑρισκομεν ἀγαθον ἀνθρωπον ἐν τω κοσμω. ὁτε οἱ ἀνθρω-

ποι κρινουσιν αλλους, λεγουσιν ότι οί μαθηται οὐ μανθα-
νουσι, των ἰατρων οἱ φιλοι ἀποθνησκουσι, οἱ τελωναι κλε-
πτουσι. εἰ τους κριτικους ἀκουετε, πιστευετε ότι οὐκ ἐστιν
ἀνθρωπος δικαιος και ἀξιος δοξης. ὁ θεος ἐστιν ἀγαθος,
οἱ ἀνθρωποι πονηροι και ὑποκριται. λαμβανουσι τα των
ἀλλων, ἐσθιουσι και πινουσι. ἀλλα ὁ θεος γινωσκει τας
ἁμαρτιας των ἀνθρωπων και σωζει αὐτους. οἱ ἀνθρωποι
ἀποθνησκουσιν ἐν ταις ἁμαρτιαις. ἀλλ᾽ ὁ θεος ἐγειρει τους
νεκρους · εἰ πιστευομεν, σωτηριαν ἐχομεν.

Note the declension of αὐτος, which is used as third
person pronoun:

	Masculine	*Feminine*	*Neuter*
Singular			
Nom.	αὐτος—he	αὐτη—she	αὐτο—it
Acc.	αὐτον—him	αὐτην—her	αὐτο—it
Gen.	αὐτου—of him, his	αὐτης—of her, hers	αὐτου—of it, its
Dat.	αὐτῳ—to him	αὐτῃ—to her	αὐτῳ—to it
Plural			
Nom.	αὐτοι—they	αὐται—they	αὐτα—they
Acc.	αὐτους—them	αὐτας—them	αὐτα—them
Gen.	αὐτων—of them	αὐτων—of them	αὐτων—of them, their
Dat.	αὐτοις—to them	αὐταις—to them	αὐτοις—to them

αλλος—" other "—is declined exactly the same. Note
particularly that the nominative singular neuter is in -o
instead of -ον.

LESSON IX

THE VERB—FUTURE TENSE

This differs from the Present only by the addition of -σ- between the stem and the ending: ἀκουω—ἀκουσω · πιστευω —πιστευσω.

If the last letter of the stem is a consonant, σ is assimilated to it:

π, πτ, β, φ plus σ becomes ψ
κ, γ, χ, σσ   ,,   σ   ,,   ξ
θ, ζ   ,,   σ   ,,   σ

Some verbs have vowel stems in ε, α or o and in this case the future lengthens the vowel to η or ω: φιλεω—φιλησω (I love), τιμαω—τιμησω (I honour), πληροω—πληρωσω (I fill). (These verbs will be dealt with more fully in Lesson XVII.)

(*Note:* Three exceptions to this last rule: καλεω—καλεσω (I call), τελεω—τελεσω (I complete), ἐαω—ἐασω (I allow).

We can therefore construct the following typical Futures:

	Diphthong stem	Consonant stem
Singular		
I	ἀκουσω	γραψω
You	ἀκουσεις	γραψεις
He	ἀκουσει	γραψει
Plural		
We	ἀκουσομεν	γραψομεν
You	ἀκουσετε	γραψετε
They	ἀκυυσουσι	γραψουσι

Vowel Stems

	(-εω)	(-αω)	(-οω)
Singular			
I	φιλησω	τιμησω	πληρωσω
You	φιλησεις	τιμησεις	πληρωσεις
He	φιλησει	τιμησει	πληρωσει
Plural			
We	φιλησομεν	τιμησομεν	πληρωσομεν
You	φιλησετε	τιμησετε	πληρωσετε
They	φιλησουσι	τιμησουσι	πληρωσουσι

The declension of the First and Second Person Pronouns is:

Nom.	I—ἐγω	We—ἡμεις
Acc.	Me—ἐμε, με	Us—ἡμας
Gen.	My—ἐμου, μου	Our—ἡμων
Dat.	To me—ἐμοι, μοι	To us—ἡμιν

		Singular	Plural
Nom.	You—	συ	ὑμεις
Acc.	You—	σε	ὑμας
Gen.	Your—	σου	ὑμων
Dat.	To you—	σοι	ὑμιν

(*Note:* The shorter forms—με, μου, μοι—do not occur at the beginning of a phrase.)

THE TEN COMMANDMENTS

ἐγω εἰμι κυριος ὁ θεος σου ὁστις (who) ἐξηγαγον (led) σε ἐκ γης Αἰγυπτου.

οὐκ ἐσονται σοι θεοι ἑτεροι πλην (except) ἐμου.

οὐ ποιησεις εἰδωλον · οὐ προσκυνησεις αὐτοις, οὐδε λατρευσεις αὐτοις · ἐγω γαρ εἰμι κυριος ὁ θεος σου, θεος ζηλωτης.

οὐ λημψει (you shall take) το ὀνομα κυριου του θεου σου ἐπι ματαιῳ (in vain)

μνησθητι (remember) την ἡμεραν του σαββατου ἁγιαζειν (to make holy) αὐτην · ἐξ ἡμερας ἐργασει (you shall work) και ποιησεις παντα (all) τα ἐργα σου. τῃ δε ἡμερᾳ τῃ ἑβδομῃ σαββατον κυριου του θεου σου · οὐ ποιησεις ἐν αὐτῃ ἐργον, συ και ὁ υἱος σου, και ἡ θυγατηρ σου, ὁ παις σου και ἡ παιδισκη σου, ὁ βους σου και το ὑποζυγιον σου, και παν κτηνος (beast) και ὁ προσηλυτης ὁ παροικων (dwelling) ἐν σοι.

τιμα (honour) τον πατερα και την μητερα σου.

οὐ μοιχευσεις · οὐ κλεψεις · οὐ φονευσεις · οὐ ψευδομαρτυρησεις.

οὐκ ἐπιθυμησεις την γυναικα του πλησιον σου κ.τ.λ.

προσκυνεω—worship
λατρευω—serve
ποιεω—do, make
φονευω—murder
μοιχευω—commit adultery
ἐπιθυμεω—desire
ἐξ—six
ἑβδομος—seventh
ζηλωτης—jealous man
σαββατον—sabbath
παις—boy, servant
παιδισκη—maidservant
βους—ox

ὑποζυγιον—animal under the yoke
προσηλυτης—stranger (cf. proselyte)
ψευδομαρτυρεω—give false evidence
ματαιος—vain
υἱος—son
θυγατηρ—daughter
ὀνομα—name
πλησιον—near-by
γυναικα—wife
πατερα—father
μητερα—mother

(These last three are in the accusative case; their declensions are given in the next lesson.)

ἐκ—out of   ἐν—in, on

κ.τ.λ. (και τα λοιπα) is the abbreviation equivalent to "etc."

Future Tenses of Liquid Verbs

Verbs whose stem ends in a liquid (λ, μ, ν, ϱ) have somewhat different forms in the Future. The Greeks did not
like the pronunciation of σ after these letters, so the σ was
dropped and an ε which combined with the ending was put
in its place. In four of the six forms the ε is absorbed into
the diphthong of the ending, -ω, -εις, -ει and -ουσι, but in
the first and second person plural it turns the short vowel
into a diphthong, ου and ει.

Words which have λλ in the Present Tense drop one λ
in the Future, whilst words which have a diphthong in the
stem before λ, ν, ϱ shorten it in the Future. Here are some
typical forms:

Present

μενω	βαλλω	ἀγγελλω	αἰρω	σπειρω
(remain)	(throw)	(announce)	(lift up)	(sow)

Future

μενω	βαλω	ἀγγελω	ἀρω	σπερω
μενεις	βαλεις	ἀγγελεις	ἀρεις	σπερεις
μενει	βαλει	ἀγγελει	ἀρει	σπερει
μενουμεν	βαλουμεν	ἀγγελουμεν	ἀρουμεν	σπερουμεν
μενειτε	βαλειτε	ἀγγελειτε	ἀρειτε	σπερειτε
μενουσι	βαλουσι	ἀγγελουσι	ἀρουσι	σπερουσι

EXERCISE VIIa

τη ἑβδομη ἡμερᾳ ἀξομεν τα παιδια εἰς τα δενδρα, και
διδαξομεν αὐτους τα μυστηρια της γης. βλεψουσι τους
καρπους και τα φυλλα. ἐν τοις ἀγροις οἱ δουλοι φυλαξουσι
τα προβατα και ὁ ἀγαθος δουλος σωσει αὐτα ἀπο των
ληστων.

EXERCISE VIIb

In the last day the judge of the world will sit in the

heavens and the angels will bring the men. You will hear the account (λογος) of your sins, and you will see the righteousness of God. He will save you from destruction and will have mercy on you. No one is worthy of his love, but we shall see his glory and shall believe in (εἰς, followed by accusative) him.

EXERCISE VIIIa

μακαριος ὁ ἀνθρωπος ὁς τηρει τας παραγγελιας του θεου · αὐτος σωσει την ψυχην αὐτου ἐν τη ἐσχατη ἡμερᾳ. ὁς δε οὐ τηρει βλεψει την ὀργην του θεου. γινωσκομεν γαρ ὁτι οἱ ἀγγελοι γραψουσι τα ἐργα των ἀνθρωπων ἐν τῳ βιβλιῳ της ζωης. ὁ θεος κρινει τον κοσμον κατα (according to) τα ἐργα αὐτων και πεμψει τους ἀνθρωπους εἰς τον μισθον. πεμψει τους ἀγαθους εἰς ζωην και τους κακους εἰς ἀπωλειαν.

EXERCISE VIIIb

The teacher will teach the students the truth, but the students will not hear. They will desire wisdom, but they will not do the deeds of wisdom. Then the teacher will say, " You will seek me, but I shall not lead you to wisdom ". The words of the teacher will remain in the hearts of the wicked students and will witness to them (αὐτοις).

φυλασσω—guard
οὐρανος—heaven
καρπος—fruit
οὐδεις--no one
ὁς--who
μισθος--reward
μακαριος—happy
ἐλεεω—have mercy on
ἀπωλεια—destruction
ζητεω—seek

ἀπο—from (followed by genitive)
τοτε—then
ἀγρος—field
πεμπω—send
μυστηριον—mystery
μαρτυρεω—witness
εἰς, προς—to (followed by accusative) (when expressing motion)

(*Note:* δε—but, γαϱ—because, for. These two words are " enclitic ", which means that they cannot come as the first words in the phrase with which they are connected, though in English they are translated first. Note that " for " in English is ambiguous, and may mean " on behalf of ", " in the interest of ", as well as " because ". γαϱ in Greek ONLY MEANS " FOR " WHEN IT IS EQUIVALENT TO " BECAUSE ".)

LESSON X

THIRD DECLENSION

The Third Declension includes all the nouns not in First or Second.

Some grammars make it very complicated and show as many as 60 types, but many of these have only minor differences, and some do not occur in the New Testament. There are really two main groups:

Group I—Consonant Stems—5 masculine or feminine types; 1 neuter.

Group II—Vowel Stems—3 masculine or feminine types; 1 neuter.

In some of the types nouns of both masculine and feminine gender are found, but some types are exclusively one or other. Neuter types are quite distinct and only have neuter nouns.

The endings of the Third Declension have the same basic form, but there are some modifications in Group II. They are as follows:

| | *Masculine and Feminine* | |
	Singular	*Plural*
Nom.	(various)	-ες
Voc.	(various)	-ες
Acc.	-α	-ας
Gen.	-ος	-ων
Dat.	-ι	-σι

Neuter

	(I)		(II)	
	Singular	*Plural*	*Singular*	*Plural*
Nom.	-μα	-ματα	-ος	-η
Voc.	-μα	-ματα	-ος	-η
Acc.	-μα	-ματα	-ος	-η
Gen.	-ματος	-ματων	-ους	-εων
Dat.	-ματι	-μασι	-ει	-εσι

To find the stems to which these endings are attached, drop the ending (-ος) of the Genitive Singular.

The Nominative Singular must be learned individually, but in most cases can be easily inferred.

Note that three endings have the same characteristic letters as First and Second Declensions—dative singular -ι; genitive plural -ων; neuter plural -α.

The Neuter nouns of Group II have vowel stems ending in -ε, and this combines with the usual Third Declension endings to produce the forms noted above.

The following words belong to the various types of Group I on page 40:

Type 1   λεων, λεοντος, ὁ—lion
              ὀδους, ὀδοντος, ὁ—tooth

Type 2   σαλπιγξ, σαλπιγγος, ἡ—trumpet
              σαρξ, σαρκος, ἡ—flesh
              γυνη, γυναικος, ἡ—woman, wife
              φλοξ, φλογος, ἡ—flame
              θριξ, τριχος, ἡ—hair

(*Note:* Vocative singular of γυνη is γυναι; dative plural of θριξ is θριξι.)

GROUP I—CONSONANT STEMS

Type No.	1	2	3	4	5	6
Nom.	ἀρχων	φυλαξ	ἐλπις	ποιμην	σωτηρ	γραμμα
Gen.	ἀρχοντος	φυλακος	ἐλπιδος	ποιμενος	σωτηρος	γραμματος
Gender	All M.	M. & F.	Usually F.	M. & F.	M. & F.	All Neuter
Meaning	ruler	guard	hope	shepherd	saviour	letter (of alphabet)
Singular						
Nom.	ἀρχων	φυλαξ	ἐλπις	ποιμην	σωτηρ	γραμμα
Voc.	ἀρχων	φυλαξ	ἐλπι	ποιμην	σωτερ	γραμμα
Acc.	ἀρχοντα	φυλακα	ἐλπιδα	ποιμενα	σωτηρα	γραμμα
Gen.	ἀρχοντος	φυλακος	ἐλπιδος	ποιμενος	σωτηρος	γραμματος
Dat.	ἀρχοντι	φυλακι	ἐλπιδι	ποιμενι	σωτηρι	γραμματι
Plural						
Nom. Voc.	ἀρχοντες	φυλακες	ἐλπιδες	ποιμενες	σωτηρες	γραμματα
Acc.	ἀρχοντας	φυλακας	ἐλπιδας	ποιμενας	σωτηρας	γραμματα
Gen.	ἀρχοντων	φυλακων	ἐλπιδων	ποιμενων	σωτηρων	γραμματων
Dat.	ἀρχουσι	φυλαξι	ἐλπισι	ποιμεσι	σωτηρσι	γραμμασι

Type 3   λαμπας, λαμπαδος, ἡ—lamp
ἐρις, ἐριδος, ἡ—strife
παις, παιδος, ὁ and ἡ—boy, girl
νυξ, νυκτος, ἡ—night (dat. plur.—νυξι)
πους, ποδος, ὁ—foot
χαρις, χαριτος, ἡ—grace

(*Note:* Accusative singular of ἐρις is ἐριν; vocative singular of παις is παι.

Accusative singular of χαρις is χαριν, except in one passage where it is χαριτα.)

Type 4   μην, μηνος, ὁ—month
εἰκων, εἰκονος, ἡ—image
ἡγεμων, ἡγεμονος, ὁ—leader
κυων, κυνος, ὁ—dog
χειμων, χειμωνος, ὁ—winter
αἰων, αἰωνος, ὁ—age
ἀμπελων, ἀμπελωνος, ὁ—vineyard
χιτων, χιτωνος, ὁ—shirt, tunic
ἀγων, ἀγωνος, ὁ—game, contest

(*Note:* The stem of κυων is κυν- and dative plural is κυσι.

There is no rule about whether a noun keeps the long vowel, like αἰων, or shortens it, like εἰκων. The difference must just be learnt.

πυρ (fire) is of this type, but is neuter, and is only found in the singular: nominative, vocative, accusative πυρ, genitive πυρος, dative πυρι.)

Type 5 (All these are partly irregular, so are given in full)

	χειρ	ἀστηρ	ἀνηρ	πατηρ	μητηρ	θυγατηρ
Nom.	χειρ	ἀστηρ	ἀνηρ	πατηρ	μητηρ	θυγατηρ
Gen.	χειρος	ἀστερος	ἀνδρος	πατρος	μητρος	θυγατρος
Gender	ἡ	ὁ	ὁ	ὁ	ἡ	ἡ
Meaning	hand	star	man	father	mother	daughter

Singular

	χειρ	ἀστηρ	ἀνηρ	πατηρ	μητηρ	θυγατηρ
Nom.	χειρ	ἀστηρ	ἀνηρ	πατηρ	μητηρ	θυγατηρ
Voc.	χειρ	ἀστηρ	ἀνερ	πατερ	μητερ	θυγατερ
Acc.	χειρα	ἀστερα	ἀνδρα	πατερα	μητερα	θυγατερα
Gen.	χειρος	ἀστερος	ἀνδρος	πατρος	μητρος	θυγατρος
Dat.	χειρι	ἀστερι	ἀνδρι	πατρι	μητρι	θυγατρι

Plural

	χειρ	ἀστηρ	ἀνηρ	πατηρ	μητηρ	θυγατηρ
Nom. Voc.	χειρες	ἀστερες	ἀνδρες	πατερες	μητερες	θυγατερες
Acc.	χειρας	ἀστερας	ἀνδρας	πατερας	μητερας	θυγατερας
Gen.	χειρων	ἀστερων	ἀνδρων	πατερων	μητερων	θυγατερων
Dat.	χερσι	ἀστρασι	ἀνδρασι	πατρασι	μητρασι	θυγατρασι

Type 6 (All Neuter)

χρημα—thing
ἁμαρτημα—sin
πνευμα—spirit, wind
θελημα—will
σπερμα—seed
ὁραμα—vision
αἱμα—blood
κριμα—judgement

ὀνομα—name
στομα—mouth
παθημα—suffering
παραπτωμα—fault
σωμα—body
βαπτισμα—baptism
ῥημα—word
σχισμα—division

These nouns are all formed from verbal stems, and indicate the *product* of the action of the verb.

In Group II, Type 1 are a number of words in -σις which are also from verbal stems and indicate the *process* of the action, e.g. from stem κρι- we get κρισις which means " act of judging ", whilst κριμα means " result of judging, verdict ". The English word " judgement " can be used in either sense, but Greek has separate words.

There is also a group of words which do not end in -μα but which otherwise have the same endings, and are also neuter:

τερας, τερατος—miracle
φως, φωτος—light
οὐς, ὠτος—ear (dative plural ὠσι) •

ὑδωρ, ὑδατος—water
ἁλας, ἁλατος—salt

The following words belong to the types of Group II:

Type 1
κρισις—judgement, ἀφεσις—forgiveness, ἀναστασις—resurrection, and many verbal nouns in -σις. All feminine.

Type 2
There are very few words of this type. ὑς,ὑος—pig, which is either masculine or feminine; σταχυς—ear of corn.

GROUP II—VOWEL STEMS

Type No.	1	2	3	4
Nom.	πολις	ἰχθυς	βασιλευς	γενος
Gen.	πολεως	ἰχθυος	βασιλεως	γενους
Gender	F.	M.	M.	N.
Meaning	city	fish	king	race, nation
Singular				
Nom.	πολις	ἰχθυς	βασιλευς	γενος
Voc.	πολι	ἰχθυ	βασιλευ	γενος
Acc.	πολιν	ἰχθυν	βασιλεα	γενος
Gen.	πολεως	ἰχθυος	βασιλεως	γενους
Dat.	πολει	ἰχθυι	βασιλει	γενει
Plural				
Nom. Voc.	πολεις	ἰχθυες	βασιλεις	γενη
Acc.	πολεις	ἰχθυας	βασιλεας (-εις)	γενη
Gen.	πολεων	ἰχθυων	βασιλεων	γενεων (γενων)
Dat.	πολεσι	ἰχθυσι	βασιλευσι	γενεσι

Type 3

Words expressing an office, such as ἱερευς—priest, γραμματευς—scribe, γονευς—parent. All masculine.

Type 4

ἐτος—year, κερδος—gain, ὁρος—mountain, σκοτος—darkness, πληθος—crowd, τελος—end. All neuter.

DO NOT MIX THESE UP WITH SECOND DECLENSION NOUNS.

EXERCISE IXa

1. οἱ μεν ἀνθρωποι ἐχουσι χειρας και ποδας, οἱ δε κυνες μονον ποδας.
2. αἱ λαμπαδες λαμπουσιν ἐν ταις χερσι των θυγατερων.
3.   A Boy's Epitaph

   δωδεκ᾽ ἐτων τον παιδα πατηρ ἀπεθηκε (laid) Φιλιππος ἐνθαδε (here) την πολλην (great) ἐλπιδα, Νικοτελην.
4. παντων χρηματων ἀνθρωπος μετρον ἐστιν.
5. ἐν τῳ Νειλῳ κροκοδειλοι πολλοι (many) εἰσιν · οἱ Αἰγυπτιοι οὐκ ἀποκτεινουσιν αὐτους, ἱερους νομιζοντες (thinking). ὁ κροκοδειλος τους του χειμωνος μηνας οὐκ ἐσθιει οὐδεν, και το πολυ (most) της ἡμερας διατριβει ἐν τῃ γῃ, την δε νυκτα ἐν τῳ ποταμῳ · θερμοτερον (warmer) γαρ ἐστι το ὑδωρ του αἰθερος (than the air— see Lesson XXI). ἐχει δε ὁ κροκοδειλος ὀφθαλμους ὑος, μεγαλους (big) ὀδοντας κατα λογον (in proportion) του σωματος. γλωσσαν δε μονον ζῳων οὐκ ἐχει, οὐδε κινει την κατω γναθον. οἱ μεν ἀλλοι φευγουσιν αὐτον, ὁ δε τροχιλος (wagtail) ἐν εἰρηνῃ ἐστιν. ὁ γαρ κροκοδειλος ἐν τῳ ποταμῳ ἐχει το στομα μεστον βδελλων (full of leeches). ἐκβας δε (coming out) εἰς την γην ἀνοιγει το στομα και ὁ τροχιλος ἐμβαινει εἰς αὐτο και καταπινει τας βδελλας · ὁ δε κροκοδειλος οὐ βλαπτει αὐτον.

ἀποκτεινω—kill οὐδεν—nothing διατριβω—spend
αἰθηρ—air κινει—moves ὀφθαλμος—eye
γναθος—(fem.) jaw κατω—lower φευγω—flee
ἀνοιγω—open ἐμβαινω—enter βλαπτω—harm
καταπινω—drink up δωδεκα—twelve μονον—only

... μεν ...,... δε.... These two words are " enclitic ", i.e. they cannot be first word in a sentence. They are used to contrast two phrases, and when preceded by an article they mean " the one ...", " the other ..."

EXERCISE IXb

A boy is a wonderful animal. When he is small he sees visions of hope and knows that he will do good things in the world. When he is a student he reads his books and learns many things (πολλα). His parents rejoice in his wisdom, and believe that he will seek glory in the world. The lamp of truth shines in his eyes, and his ears hear the voice of knowledge. He is a leader of the contest and his name is in the mouths of men. When he finds a wife he leaves his father and mother, and watches over her. He guards her image in his heart and rejoices in her grace. The power of his body is strong, but it does not remain, and the end of a man draws near. His hair is white, he has no teeth and the flame of his spirit dies in the darkness.

wonderful—θαυμαστος read—ἀναγινωσκω
knowledge—γνωσις, -εως, ἡ leave—καταλειπω
power—δυναμις, -εως, ἡ draw near—ἐγγιζω
white—λευκος strong—ἰσχυρος

LESSON XI

THE VERB—PAST TENSES

You have seen how the Future Tense is formed by adding -σ- to the stem of the Present. The Simple Past Tense, which is called the AORIST (unlimited) also has the additional -σ- but its endings mostly have -α- in them. You must also look at the beginning of the word as well as the end. The Future, like the donkey, has a tail added; the Past is like the elephant, with a trunk as well! The " trunk " is the letter ε which is placed before the stem, and is called the AUGMENT.

For example, the Aorist of πιστευω is:

ἐπιστευσα—I believed	ἐπιστευσαμεν—we believed
ἐπιστευσας—you believed	ἐπιστευσατε—you believed
ἐπιστευσε(ν)—he believed	ἐπιστευσαν—they believed

Note the following points:

1. 2nd person singular still ends in -ς.
   1st person plural still ends in -μεν.
   2nd person plural still ends in -τε.
2. The same rules about consonant stems which were given for the Future also apply to the Aorist, e.g. βλεπω—ἐβλεψα, γραφω—ἐγραψα, διδασκω—ἐδιδαξα, λεγω—ἐλεξα.
3. Verbs with stems in ε, α, or ο, lengthen the vowel, as the Future, e.g. φιλεω—ἐφιλησα, τιμαω—ἐτιμησα, πληροω—ἐπληρωσα (see Lesson XVII).
4. The Augment is always added to the front of a Past Tense, and if the verb begins with a vowel the Augment combines with it, according to the following rules:

47

ε—α becomes η, e.g. ἀκουω becomes ἤκουσα

ε—ε „ η, „ ἐγειρω „ ἤγειρα

ε—ο „ ω, „ ὁμολογεω (I confess)
becomes ὡμολογησα

ε—αι „ η, „ αἰτεω (I ask) becomes
ᾔτησα

ε—οι „ ῳ, „ οἰκεω (I dwell) „
ᾤκησα

Note that the iota is written subscript.

5. In a verb which is compounded with a preposition Augment goes *after* the preposition, and *before* the main verb. Since most of the prepositions end in a vowel this also brings two vowels together, but in this case THE LAST VOWEL OF THE PREPOSITION IS DROPPED, except in the case of three prepositions περι, προ, ἀμφι (see Lesson XXII).

So far you have had the following compound verbs. See how the Augment is added in each of these cases:

απο|κτεινω—ἀπ|εκτεινα   προσ|κυνεω—προσ|εκυνησα
ἀπο|στελλω—ἀπ|εστειλα   κατα|κρινω—κατ|εκρινα
ἐπι|θυμεω—ἐπ|εθυμησα   δια|τριβω—δι|ετριψα

6. The Liquid Verbs (with stems in λ, μ, ν, ρ) have similar peculiarities in the Aorist as in the Future, since they have no -σ-. Also they strengthen the vowel of the stem when possible, but their endings are the same as the regular verb:

μενω—ἔμεινα   αἰρω—ἦρα
κρινω—ἔκρινα   σπειρω—ἔσπειρα
κτεινω—ἔκτεινα   ἐγειρω—ἤγειρά
στελλω—ἔστειλα   φθειρω (I destroy)--ἔφθειρα
ἀγγελλω—ἤγγειλα

The Imperfect Tense

The Aorist merely says that something happened in the Past, without any further limitation (" I did "). There is another tense which is used for an action which was either CONTINUOUS (" I was doing "), or REPEATED (" I used to do ") or HABITUAL. This is called the Imperfect, and is formed from the Present, with the Augment added to show that it is Past. The vowels in the ending are ε and ο as in the Present, and all the endings are short.

Singular

ἐπιστευον—I was believing
ἐπιστευες—you were believing
ἐπιστευε(ν)—he was believing

Plural

ἐπιστευομεν—we were believing
ἐπιστευετε—you were believing
ἐπιστευον—they were believing

It is important to distinguish these two tenses and to note that unless there is a need to emphasize that an action is continuous or habitual, Greek prefers to use the Aorist.

The Second (Strong) Aorist

In English the Past Tense may be formed in one of two ways:

1. By adding -ed to the stem, e.g. I live—I lived; I hope—I hoped; I save—I saved.
2. By strengthening the stem vowel, e.g. I sing—I sang; I give—I gave; I bring—I brought.

This second form is called the STRONG or SECOND AORIST, in contrast to the WEAK or FIRST AORIST, which just adds -ed.

The same two types are found in Greek, and as in English, there is no rule about which type a particular verb uses, so they must be learned individually. The endings are like the Imperfect, the difference being in the stem.

The following are the most common SECOND AORISTS:

Present	Imperfect	Second Aorist	Meaning
βαλλω	ἐβαλλον	ἐβαλον	throw
ἁμαρτανω	ἡμαρτανον	ἡμαρτον	sin
λαμβανω	ἐλαμβανον	ἐλαβον	take, receive
μανθανω	ἐμανθανον	ἐμαθον	learn
πινω	ἐπινον	ἐπιον	drink
ἀπο-θνησκω	ἀπ-εθνησκον	ἀπ-εθανον	die
εὑρισκω	εὑρισκον	εὑρον [ηὑρον]	find
πιπτω	ἐπιπτον	ἐπεσον	fall
τικτω	ἐτικτον	ἐτεκον	bring forth child
κατα-λειπω	κατ-ελειπον	κατ-ελιπον	leave
φευγω	ἐφευγον	ἐφυγον	run away, flee
ἀγω	ἠγον	ἠγαγον	lead
γινωσκω	ἐγινωσκον	ἐγνων	know
βαινω	ἐβαινον	ἐβην	go
[ὁραω]	(see Lesson XVII)	εἰδον	see
[λεγω]	ἐλεγον	εἰπον	say
[ἐχω]	εἰχον	ἐσχον	have
[ἐσθιω]	ἠσθιον	ἐφαγον	eat
[πασχω]	ἐπασχον	ἐπαθον	suffer
[ἐρχομαι]	(see Lesson XIV)	ἠλθον	come, go
[φερω]	ἐφερον	ἠνεγκον	carry

The last seven verbs are DEFECTIVE, that is to say, the

Aorist is formed from a different stem from the Present. Originally there were two verbs of similar meaning, and parts of each have got lost, and the remaining parts put together as though they were one verb.

The Aorists of γινωσκω, and βαινω are irregular:

ἐγνων, ἐγνως, ἐγνω, ἐγνωμεν, ἐγνωτε, ἐγνωσαν
ἐβην, ἐβης, ἐβη, ἐβημεν, ἐβητε, ἐβησαν

EXERCISE Xa. THE GOVERNOR

ὁ ἡγεμων ἦν καλος και ἀγαθος ἀνηρ. τα χρηματα οὐκ ἐτηρησεν ἐν ταις χερσιν αὐτου, ἀλλ' ἐβοηθησε τοις μαθηταις. ἡ μητηρ του πατρος αὐτου ἐλαμβανε πεντε ἀργυρια κατα μηνας (monthly) ἀπο των της πολεως εὐαγγελιστων και οἱ εὐαγγελισται ἐδιδασκον τον πατερα δωρεαν (freely). δια τουτο (therefore), ὁ ἡγεμων εἰπεν ὁτι αὐτοι ἠσαν σωτηρες του πατρος και ἐτιμησεν αὐτους. ἐν τη του δημου ἐκκλησια ἐμαρτυρησε την πιστιν, και ᾐτησεν ἐλευθεριαν τοις χριστιανοις. πεντε ἐτη ἡγεμονευε της ἐπαρχιας και παντες (all men) ἐφιλησαν αὐτον και ἐτιμησαν αὐτον. το ὀνομα αὐτου ἦν ἐν τοις του πληθους στομασι και το τελος αὐτου ἐπληρωσεν αὐτους λυπης.

βοηθεω—help (followed by dative)
ἐλευθερια—freedom
ἐπαρχια—province
πιστις, -εως, ἡ—faith
τιμαω—honour
πεντε—five
αἰτεω—ask for
παντες—all men
δημος—people
πληροω—I fill

EXERCISE Xb

His parents sent the boy to the city because there was no work in the vineyard. In his hand was a little money, and in his heart was hope. He walked along the road by night (νυκτος) and saw the stars in the heavens. In the

city he sought the house of a priest and asked for food,
but the priest did not help him. The dogs barked and
seized his garment, but he struck their mouths and they
were silent. In another house he saw the flame of a fire
and a lamp by the side of an image, and he asked for bread
and water. He heard the voice of a woman in the house,
and she said to her daughter, " Give (δος) bread to the
boy ".

ὀλίγος—little　　βρωμα—food　　φωνεω—bark
σιωπαω—be silent　　περι|πατεω—walk
παρα—followed by the accusative case means "along"
　　　　followed by the dative case means " by the side of "
　　　　(see Lesson XXII).

EXERCISE XIa.　A　FABLE　OF　AESOP

κυων ὁς κρεας ἐφερε, ποταμον διεβαινε. ὁτε δε εἰδε την
ἑαυτου σκιαν ἐπι του ὑδατος ὑπελαβεν ὁτι ἑτερος κυων ἐστι
και κρεας ἐχει. ἀπεβαλεν οὐν το ἰδιον κρεας και το του
ἑτερου ἡρπαζε ὡστε ἀπωλεσεν (he lost) ἀμφοτερα. το μεν
γαρ οὐκ ἠν, το δε εἰς τον ποταμον ἐπεσε.

κρεας, κρεατος, το—meat　　ἑαυτον, ἑαυτου, ἑαυτῳ—himself
σκια, σκιας, ἡ—shadow　　ὑπο|λαμβανω—think, conjecture
ἀμφοτερος—both　　ὡστε—so that
οὐν—therefore (enclitic)

EXERCISE XIb

The king went to another city and left his money in the
hands of his servants. One servant received ten talents,
another five and another two. The king remained in the
other city for six months and then returned to his house.
He called his servants who (οἱ) came and brought the
talents. The first servant said, " See, I received ten talents
and now I have twenty ". The second servant said, " See,

I received five talents, and now I have ten ". The king
honoured the good servants who (οἱ) brought back the
money. The third servant said, " I knew that the king had
much (πολλα) money, so I ate and drank and now I have
nothing (οὐδεν) ". The king said, " You wicked servant,
who (ὅς) did not learn wisdom ", and threw him out of the
city.

ταλαντον—talent (£240)   ὑπ|αγω—return
ἀνα|φερω—bring back   ἐκ|βαλλω—throw out
νυν—now   ἰδου—see
δυο—two   πεντε—five   ἑξ—six   δεκα—ten
εἰκοσι—twenty

LESSON XII

INFINITIVES AND PARTICIPLES

1. *Infinitives*

I like <u>to teach</u> (general)   θελω <u>διδασκειν</u>
You like <u>to learn</u> (general)   θελετε <u>μανθανειν</u>
I want <u>to teach</u> this (particular)   θελω <u>διδαξαι</u> τουτο
You want <u>to learn</u> this (particular)   θελετε <u>μαθειν</u> τουτο

English has only one Infinitive, but Greek has four, though only two are common in the New Testament. In the above sentences are the Present Infinitive (in the first pair) and the Aorist Infinitive (in the second pair). The difference between them is not a matter of time, but of THE KIND OF ACT. The Present Infinitive is ONLY used to emphasize that the action is *continuous* or *habitual*, and therefore the Aorist Infinitive is more common in Greek. It is a safe rule—" When in doubt use the Aorist Infinitive."

The Aorist Infinitive has no Augment, since it does not refer to Past time.

The Subject of the Infinitive is usually in the Accusative Case.

The negative of the Infinitive is μη instead of οὐ.

The endings of the Infinitive in the Active are:

Present Infinitive   .   .   ειν—λυειν (to loosen)
1st Aorist Infinitive   .   .   σαι—λυσαι („   „)
2nd Aorist Infinitive   .   .   ειν—μαθειν (to learn)
Future Infinitive   .   .   σειν—λυσειν (to be
    (but his is rare)   about to loosen)

The Infinitve of εἰμι is εἰναι, and the Second Aorist

Infinitives of γινωσκω and βαινω are γνωναι and βηναι respectively.

(*Note:* This is your first introduction to the Greek " pattern verb "—λυω (I loosen)—which is used in all grammar books as an example. It is not one of the commonest verbs in the New Testament, but it has the great virtue of being completely regular, and also short. You will now meet it frequently and should get to know it thoroughly.)

EXERCISE XIIa

καλον ἐστιν ἀνθρωπον φαγειν και πιειν ὁτι ἐλαβε το σωμα ἀπο του θεου. καλον ἐστι ζητησαι την σοφιαν ὁτι ὁ σοφος γινωσκει τα μυστηρια του κοσμου. εἰ δε θελεις μαθειν την ἀληθειαν, δει σε αἰτησαι τον θεον βοηθησαι σοι. ὁ ἀνθρωπος οὐ δυνατος ἐστιν εὑρειν την δικαιοσυνην ἐν τῳ κοσμῳ. θελει ποιησαι το ἀγαθον ἀλλα οὐ θελει τηρειν τας ἐντολας του θεου. θελει γνωναι την ἀληθειαν ἀλλ᾿ οὐ θελει καταλιπειν τα ἰδια νοηματα και ποιησαι το θελημα του θεου. το θελημα του θεου ἐστιν ἀγαθον και ποιειν αὐτο ἐστι ζωη τοις ἀνθρωποις. ἡ μεν ἁμαρτια μενει ἐν τοις ἀνθρωποις ὡστε αὐτους ἀποθανειν. ἡ δε ἀγαπη του θεου σωζει αὐτους ὡστε εἰσελθειν εἰς την βασιλειαν αὐτου.

δει—it is necessary   δυνατος—able, possible
νοημα—thought

ὡστε followed by Accusative and Infinitive, expresses result —" so that ".

EXERCISE XIIb

If you wish to do good, it is necessary to keep the commandments of God, and the first commandment is to love men. Jesus spoke a parable about love. He said that to love men * was to help them. The priest and the Levite were not willing to help the man, but the Samaritan carried him to the inn and told the innkeeper to care for him. The will of the Samaritan was to do good to the man, and thus he kept the commandments of God.

about—περι (with genitive) be willing—θελω, aorist
inn—πανδοχειον ηθελησα
thus—ούτως Samaritan—Σαμαρειτης
Jesus—'Ιησους care for—θεραπευω
Levite—Λευΐτης love—use φιλεω
innkeeper—πανδοχευς

(*Note:* * When spoken words are reported in Greek the tense of the verb does *not* depend on the verb of speaking, as in English. The tense of the original saying is retained. In this paragraph the original saying is " to love men *is* to help them ", but in English " is " becomes " was " after " said ", which is a Past tense. In Greek *this does not happen*, but " is " remains " is ".)

2. *Participles*

Consider the following verse:

" A fellow-feeling makes us wondrous kind "
Methinks the poet would have changed his mind
If he had found some fellow feeling in his coat behind.

Clearly " fellow-feeling " does not quite mean the same in the first and third lines. Why? Because " fellow " in the first line is an adjective describing " feeling ", and in the third line it is a noun. Further, " feeling " in the first line is a noun, whilst in the third line it is a PARTICIPLE, which (*a*) says something about the fellow, and therefore has the force of an adjective, and (*b*) describes an action, and therefore has the force of a verb. It is therefore called a VERBAL ADJECTIVE.

In English there are only two Participles, the Present Participle in -ing, and the Past Participle in -ed, the former being active and the latter passive, but the use of participles is very loose, e.g.

1. She went out *crying* bitterly.
2. *Saying* " BAH ", he turned and dashed out.

The two forms are exactly the same, but obviously in the first case the lady's crying went on for some time, whereas in the second case the whole effect of " BAH " demands a short, sharp word. Also the time is different, since the lady's crying was simultaneous with her going out, whereas the man's exclamation came first, and then he went out.

The Greeks were more careful and used participles accurately; each of the four participles has its proper use, at the proper time.

> The *Present Participle* refers to an action *simultaneous with* the main verb.
>
> The *Future Participle* refers to an action *after* the main verb (but this is very rare in N.T. Greek).
>
> The *Aorist Participle* refers to an action *before* the main verb.
>
> The *Perfect Participle* (see next lesson) refers to a *state* simultaneous with the main verb, which has resulted from an action before it.

(*Note specially:* the time reference of the Participle is always RELATIVE TO THE MAIN VERB.)

The Participle is an *adjective*, so like all adjectives it must agree with the noun to which it refers in number, gender and case.

The Participle is a *verb* and so it may govern an object, like any other part of the verb.

The negative used with the Participle is μη, not οὐ.

Examples:

1. The man, crossing the river, saw a dog.
   ὁ ἀνθρωπος, διαβαινων τον ποταμον, εἰδε κυνα
2. The man saw a dog crossing the river.
   ὁ ἀνθρωπος εἰδε κυνα διαβαινοντα τον ποταμον.
3. The woman, crossing the river, saw a sheep.
   ἡ γυνη διαβαινουσα τον ποταμον εἰδε προβατον.
4. The woman saw a sheep crossing the river.
   ἡ γυνη εἰδε προβατον διαβαινον τον ποταμον.
5. The sheep of the man crossing the river was white.
   το προβατον του διαβαινοντος τον ποταμον ἠν λευκον.

Declension of Participles. In the Masculine and Neuter the Participle has Third Declension endings, and in the Feminine it has First Declension endings of the α-impure type:

| | *Present type* | | |
	Masc.	*Fem.*	*Neut.*
Singular			
Nom.	λυ-ων	λυ-ουσα	λυ-ον
Voc.	λυ-ων	λυ-ουσα	λυ-ον
Acc.	λυ-οντα	λυ-ουσαν	λυ-ον
Gen.	λυ-οντος	λυ-ουσης	λυ-οντος
Dat.	λυ-οντι	λυ-ουσῃ	λυ-οντι
Plural			
Nom.	λυ-οντες	λυ-ουσαι	λυ-οντα
Acc.	λυ-οντας	λυ-ουσας	λυ-οντα
Gen.	λυ-οντων	λυ-ουσων	λυ-οντων
Dat.	λυ-ουσι	λυ-ουσαις	λυ-ουσι

First Aorist type

	Masc.	Fem.	Neut.
Singular			
Nom.	λυ-σ-ας	λυ-σ-ασα	λυ-σ-αν
Voc.	λυ-σ-ας	λυ-σ-ασα	λυ-σ-αν
Acc.	λυ-σ-αντα	λυ-σ-ασαν	λυ-σ-αν
Gen.	λυ-σ-αντος	λυ-σ-ασης	λυ-σ-αντος
Dat.	λυ-σ-αντι	λυ-σ-αση	λυ-σ-αντι
Plural			
Nom.	λυ-σ-αντες	λυ-σ-ασαι	λυ-σ-αντα
Acc.	λυ-σ-αντας	λυ-σ-ασας	λυ-σ-αντα
Gen.	λυ-σ-αντων	λυ-σ-ασων	λυ-σ-αντων
Dat.	λυ-σ-ασι	λυ-σ-ασαις	λυ-σ-ασι

(*Note:* The Participle of εἰμι is ὤν, οὖσα, ὄν.

The Aorist Participle of γινωσκω is γνους, γνουσα, γνον.

The Aorist Participle of βαινω is βας, βασα, βαν.

The endings of the Future Participle and of the Second Aorist Participle are exactly the same as the Present, but the stem, of course, is different.)

EXERCISE XIIIa

και ἠν ἀνηρ ἐν Βαβυλωνι και ὀνομα αὐτῳ Ἰωακειμ. και ἐλαβεν γυναικα ᾑ ὀνομα Σουσαννα, θυγατηρ Χελκειου, καλη και εὐσεβουσα τον Κυριον. και οἱ γονεις αὐτης ἠσαν δικαιοι και ἐδιδαξαν την θυγατερα αὐτων κατα τον νομον Μωυσεως. και δυο πρεσβυτεροι ἐλθοντες εἰς τον οἰκον Ἰωακειμ και ἰδοντες την γυναικα περιπατουσαν ἐν τῳ παραδεισῳ του ἀνδρος αὐτης και ἐπιθυμησαντες αὐτης ἐξεκλιναν τους ὀφθαλμους αὐτων ποιησαι κακα. και ἠλθεν ἡ γυνη εἰς τον παραδεισον και οἱ δυο πρεσβυτεροι ἠσαν βλεποντες αὐτην.

EXERCISE XIIIb

The wicked elders, coming into the assembly, said that
the woman was speaking with a young man, but they,
turning him out of the garden, seized her. Hearing the
words of the elders, the people condemned Susanna to die,
but Daniel, jumping up, cried, " I am innocent of the blood
of the woman ". Then he commanded the first elder to
say where the woman was speaking with the young man,
and he said " Under a fig-tree ". Then he asked the
second elder, and he said to him " Under an olive-tree ".
But Daniel, hearing, said, " The two elders are speaking
lies ", and so he saved the woman.

turn out—$\dot{\varepsilon}\varkappa$ | $\beta\alpha\lambda\lambda\omega$

seize—$\varkappa\rho\alpha\tau\varepsilon\omega$

cry out—$\beta o\alpha\omega$

where—$\dot{o}\pi ov$

olive-tree—$\dot{\varepsilon}\lambda\alpha\iota\alpha$, -$\alpha\varsigma$, $\dot{\eta}$

reverence—$\varepsilon\dot{v}\sigma\varepsilon\beta\varepsilon\omega$

bend—$\dot{\varepsilon}\varkappa$ | $\varkappa\lambda\iota\nu\omega$

under—$\dot{v}\pi o$ followed by dative (Lesson XXII)

speak—$\lambda\varepsilon\gamma\omega$

with—$\mu\varepsilon\tau\alpha$ followed by genitive (Lesson XXII)

condemn—$\varkappa\alpha\tau\alpha$ | $\varkappa\rho\iota\nu\omega$

jump up—$\dot{\alpha}\nu\alpha$ | $\pi\eta\delta\alpha\omega$

innocent—$\dot{\alpha}\theta\omega o\varsigma$

fig-tree—$\sigma v\varkappa\eta$, -$\eta\varsigma$, $\dot{\eta}$

lie—$\psi\varepsilon v\delta o\varsigma$, -$ov\varsigma$, τo

garden—$\pi\alpha\rho\alpha\delta\varepsilon\iota\sigma o\varsigma$

desire—$\dot{\varepsilon}\pi\iota$ ' $\theta v\mu\varepsilon\omega$

according to—$\varkappa\alpha\tau\alpha$

command—$\varkappa\varepsilon\lambda\varepsilon v\omega$

Daniel—$\varDelta\alpha\nu\iota\eta\lambda$

ask (question)—$\dot{\varepsilon}\rho\omega\tau\alpha\omega$

LESSON XIII

THE VERB—PERFECT AND PLUPERFECT TENSES

The Perfect Tense describes a PRESENT STATE OR CONDITION, resulting from a Past Action;
The Pluperfect Tense describes a PAST STATE OR CONDITION, resulting from an action prior to it.

It must always be remembered that the Perfect Tense is PRIMARILY concerned with the PRESENT time, e.g.

τεθνηκε the perfect of ἀποθνησκω does not mean " he died ", but " he *is now* dead ".
γεγραφα the perfect of γραφω means " it *is there* on the blackboard, because I wrote it ".

The Perfect is formed by a kind of stutter, in which the first consonant of the word, followed by ε, is put in front of the stem. This is called REDUPLICATION, e.g.

> πιστευω—πεπιστευκα
> σωζω—σεσωκα
> τιμαω—τετιμηκα
> λυω—λελυκα
> μαρτυρεω (bear witness)—μεμαρτυρηκα
> δουλοω (enslave)—δεδουλωκα

When the first letter is an aspirated letter, the equivalent unaspirated letter is used in the reduplication, e.g.

> φιλεω—πεφιληκα   θεωρεω—τεθεωρηκα

When the first letter of the stem is a vowel, it is lengthened in place of the reduplication, e.g.

61

αἰτεω—ἤτηκα   ἀγαπαω (love)—ἠγαπηκα

The distinguishing letters of the Perfect ending are κα-.

	Singular	*Plural*
1st person	λε-λυ-κα—I have loosed	λε-λυ-καμεν—we have loosed
2nd person	λε-λυ-κας etc.	λε-λυ-κατε, etc.
3rd person	λϑ-λυ-κε	λε-λυ-κασι

Infinitive—λελυκεναι
Participle—λελυκως,   λελυκυια,   λελυκος
    (gen.)—λελυκοτος,   λελυκυιας,   λελυκοτος

Second (Strong) Perfects

Just as there are Second Aorists, there are also Second Perfects, or " Strong Perfects ". The endings are the same, except that κ is omitted. The most common of these are:

ἀκουω—ἀκηκοα   γραφω—γεγραφα
κραζω (cry out)—κεκραγα   κρυπτω (hide)—κεκρυφα
πασχω—πεπονθα   λαμβανω—εἰληφα

Note also: γεγονα—I have become, I am
           ἐληλυθα—I have come, I am here
           πεποιθα—I trust, I am confident
           ὁραω—ἑωρακα   [λεγω]—εἰρηκα

The Pluperfect is not very frequent, even in Classical Greek, but it does occur a few times in the New Testament. It is a past tense like the Aorist and Imperfect, therefore has an Augment as well as reduplication, though there are some examples in the New Testament where the Augment is omitted. The characteristic letters are κει.

	Singular	Plural
1st person	ἐ-λε-λυ-κειν—I had loosed	ἐ-λε-λυ-κειμεν—we had loosed
2nd person	ἐ-λε-λυ-κεις etc.	ἐ-λε-λυ-κειτε etc.
3rd person	ἐ-λε-λυ-κει	ἐ-λε-λυ-κεισαν [ἐλελυκεσαν]

(*Note:* The Pluperfect is NEVER used as though it were a simple past tense, as is done in some Indian languages.)

EXERCISE XIVa

1. λεγει αὐτῳ ὁ Ἰησους, ὁτι ἑωρακας με, πεπιστευκας; μακαριοι οἱ μη ἰδοντες και πιστευσαντες.
2. ὁτε δε γεγονα ἀνηρ, κατηργηκα τα του νηπιου.
3. Ἰουδαιους οὐκ ἠδικηκα, ὡς συ καλως γινωσκεις.
4. πειρασμος ὑμας οὐκ εἰληφεν, εἰ μη ἀνθρωπινος.
5. ὁ γαρ θεος εἰρηκε δια στοματος των προφητων.
6. Ἑλληνας εἰσηγαγεν εἰς το ἱερον και κεκοινωκεν τον ἁγιον τοπον.
7. και ἀπελθουσα εἰς τον οἰκον εἰδεν το δαιμονιον ἐξεληλυθος ἐκ του παιδιου.
8. ἠγγικεν ἡ βασιλεια του θεου.
9. ὁ γεγραφα, γεγραφα.
10. κυριε, ἐν σοι πεποιθαμεν.

EXERCISE XIVb

1. I have learned the words well.
2. Now that you have become a man, you ought to teach others.
3. The Lord has spoken evil about you.
4. I have told you the words of truth, but you have not believed.
5. What we have seen and heard we declare to you.

6. The evil spirit has seized the boy.
7. You have filled Jerusalem with your teaching.
8. The teacher has come and the students must listen to him.

> κατ | αϱγεω—do away with, cancel
> ἀδικεω—injure
> κοινοω—make common, defile
> ὁ—what (relative; Lesson XXIV)
> πληϱοω—fill
> ʿΙεϱουσαλημ, ἡ (indeclinable)—Jerusalem
> διδαχη—teaching
> νηπιος—child, infant
> πειϱασμος—testing
> ἀνθϱωπινος—on a human scale
> εἰ μη—if not, except
> τοπος—place
> ὡς—as
> καλως—well

THE VERB—MIDDLE VOICE

In English, verbs have two voices, Active and Passive, e.g. the boy leads the dog—the dog is led by the boy. In the former the subject does an action, in the latter the subject has something done to it. Greek has another voice called the MIDDLE VOICE, in which the subject both acts and is acted upon, i.e. the subject acts directly or indirectly upon itself. This happens in various ways:

1. *Reflexive*
   ἐνδύω—I put on (someone else)
   ἐνδυομαι—I put on (myself)
   λουω—I wash (someone else)
   λουομαι—I wash (myself)
2. *Indirect Reflexive*—I do something for my own interest
   μεταπεμπω—I send A after B
   μεταπεμπομαι—I send A to bring B—I summon B
3. *Intransitive*
   παυω—I stop (someone else)
   παυομαι—I stop (myself), I cease
4. *Causative*—I get something done for myself (this is rare in N.T.)
5. *Reciprocal*
   ἀσπαζονται—They greet one another
   διαλεγονται—They talk to one another, discuss

In some words the Middle has developed into almost a different meaning, e.g.

καταλαμβανω—I seize
καταλαμβανομαι—I seize with the mind, I comprehend

65

πειθω—I persuade
πειθομαι—I submit to persuasion, I obey
ἀποδιδωμι—I give away
ἀποδιδομαι—I give away for myself, I sell

There are some verbs which have only the Middle or Passive Voice in use, and these are called DEPONENT VERBS, since they are thought of as having " put aside " (from Latin—depono, I put aside) the Active. The most common are:

γινομαι—I become
βουλομαι—I wish
ἐρχομαι—I come
ἁπτομαι—I touch (followed by genitive)
εὐ | αγγελιζομαι—I preach the gospel

δεομαι—I beseech
δεχομαι—I receive
ἀρχομαι—I begin
ἀπο | κρινομαι—I answer
ἐργαζομαι—I work
πορευομαι—I go, travel
δυναμαι—I am able, I can

(*Note:* δυναμαι has -α- in all the endings in place of -ο- or -ε- and it is followed by a verb in the infinitive.)

δεομαι, πορευομαι, δυναμαι have Passive form of Aorist stem. ἀποκρινομαι has both Middle and Passive forms.

μαχομαι—I fight

ὀργιζομαι—I am angry

The Middle endings are:

Present	Imperfect	Future	1st Aorist
λυ-ομαι	ἐ-λυ-ομην	λυ-σ-ομαι	ἐ-λυ-σ-αμην
λυ-ει, λυ-η	ἐ-λυ-ου	λυ-σ-ει, λυση	ἐ-λυ-σ-ω
λυ-εται	ἐ-λυ-ετο	λυ-σ-εται	ἐ-λυ-σ-ατο
λυ-ομεθα	ἐ-λυ-ομεθα	λυ-σ-ομεθα	ἐ-λυ-σ-αμεθα
λυ-εσθε	ἐ-λυ-εσθε	λυ-σ-εσθε	ἐ-λυ-σ-ασθε
λυ-ονται	ἐ-λυ-οντο	λυ-σ-ονται	ἐ-λυ-σ-αντο

Future and Aorist Middle of Liquid Verbs are formed as noted for the Active on pp. 35 and 48.

Verbs which have Second Aorists in the Active also have Second Aorists in the Middle, and they are formed from the same stem as the Active: endings are like Imperfect.

λαμβανω—ἐλαβον—ἐλαβομην
λειπω—ἐλιπον—ἐλιπομην
βαλλω—ἐβαλον—ἐβαλομην

Also γινομαι has Second Aorist, ἐγενομην.

Infinitives

Present	λυ-εσθαι	Future	λυ-σ-εσθαι
1st Aorist	λυ-σ-ασθαι	2nd Aorist	λαβ-εσθαι

Participles (declined like κακος)

Present	λυ-ομενος	Future	λυ-σ-ομενος
1st Aorist	λυ-σ-αμενος	2nd Aorist	λαβ-ομενος

EXERCISE XVa

δεκα μεν ἐτη ἐμαχοντο περι την Τροιαν οἱ Ἑλληνες, και ὁ Ἀγαμεμνων και ὁ Ἀχιλλευς, ὀντες ἡγεμονες των Ἑλληνων, διεφεροντο ἀλληλοις περι παρθενου. ὁπως δε τουτο ἐγενετο, εὐθυς ἀκουσεσθε. Χρυσης, ὁ του Ἀπολλωνος ἱερευς, ἐβουλετο ἀνακομιζεσθαι (to get back) την παρθενον αὐτου ἡν (whom) ἐλαβε ὁ Ἀγαμεμνων, ἀλλα ὁ Ἀγαμεμνων οὐκ ἐδεξατο τα δωρα αὐτου και εἰπεν, ἡμεις Ἑλληνες οὐ ματην μαχομεθα. εἰ κορην φερομεθα, οὐκ ἀποπεμπομεθα. οὑτως ὠργιζετο ὁ Ἀπολλων τοις Ἑλλησιν ὡστε νυκτος ἐρχομενος πολλους διειργασατο (destroyed). ὁ δε Καλχας ὁ προφητης εἰπε, συ, ὦ Ἀγαμεμνων, οὐκ ἐδεξω τα δωρα, οὐδε ἐλυσας την του ἱερεως θυγατερα. εἰ ἀποπεμψει αὐτην, παντα καλως ἐσται. ὁ οὐν Ἀγαμεμνων ἀπεκρινατο, την παρθενον ἀποπεμψομαι και την Βρισηιδα την του Ἀχιλλεως κορην, λημψομαι. οὑτως, κατα τον Ὁμηρον, ἠρξατο ἡ του Ἀχιλλεως μηνις (wrath).

'Ελλην—Greek
ματην—in vain
εὐθυς—immediately
ἀλληλους—one another
δωρον—gift
ὑπακουω—obey (+ dative)
διαφερομαι—differ
ὁπως—how

λημψομαι is future of λαμβανω, in active sense

νυκτος—by night (the genitive case is used to express " time during which " something happens)

ἀκολουθεω—follow (+ dative)

EXERCISE XVb

When the apostles began to preach the Gospel to the Greeks, they received it with joy. Paul went to Athens and spoke to the wise men in the Areopagus. Then he went to Corinth and worked with Aquila. The city of Corinth was wicked but many (πολλοι) of the Corinthians believed. Paul was able to persuade them to follow the Lord, and they were obeying his words. They put on themselves the spirit of righteousness, and baptized themselves in the name of the Lord.

(Look up the Proper Names for this piece in the Book of Acts.)

LESSON XV

THE VERB—PASSIVE VOICE

In the Active Voice the subject *does something* to someone, he acts.

In the Passive Voice the subject *has something done* to him *by* someone else, *with* something, e.g.

Active—The man strikes the dog.
Passive—The dog is struck *by* the man *with* a stick.

The person *by whom* the act is done is called the AGENT, and is expressed in Greek by ὑπο followed by a Genitive case.

The thing *with which* the act is done is called the INSTRUMENT, and is expressed in Greek by the Dative case, sometimes with ἐν.

(*Note:* THE AGENT MUST BE *LIVING* AND IS PRECEDED BY ὑπο.)

The forms of the Passive Tenses are as follows:

Present and Imperfect. These are exactly like the Present and Imperfect Middle, so you do not have anything new to learn.

Future. This must be carefully watched. It is not formed from the Present, like other Futures, but from the Aorist Passive. If the Aorist Passive is a First Aorist, then the Future is a First Future, and if the Aorist is Second, then the Future is Second. In either case it is formed by dropping the Augment, and the final ν of the Aorist and adding -σομαι. The endings are then the same as the Future Middle.

69

Aorist. This has endings which are more like Active endings. The characteristic letters of the First Aorist are -θη-.

1st Aorist		Future	
ἐ-λυ-θην	ἐ-λυ-θημεν	λυ-θη-σομαι	λυ-θη-σομεθα
ἐ-λυ-θης	ἐ-λυ-θητε	λυ-θη-σει [η]	λυ-θη-σεσθε
ἐ-λυ-θη	ἐ-λυ-θησαν	λυ-θη-σεται	λυ-θη-σονται

If the last letter of the stem is a consonant, it is modified before θ as follows:

π, πτ, β	become φ
κ, γ, χ, ξ, σσ	become χ
θ, ζ	become σ
ν	disappears

but these should all be checked with the list of verbs, as some are irregular.

Second Aorist. A few verbs have Second Aorist, which omits -θ- but otherwise is the same as First Aorist. The most common are:

ἀγγελλω—ἠγγελην	-στελλω—-εσταλην
γραφω—ἐγραφην	κρυπτω—ἐκρυβην
σπειρω—ἐσπαρην	φθειρω—ἐφθαρην
στρεφω (turn)—ἐστραφην	

Perfect and Pluperfect. These have the same endings in both Middle and Passive. They have reduplication, as in the Active, and the Pluperfect has the Augment.

Perfect		Pluperfect	
λε-λυ-μαι	λε-λυ-μεθα	ἐ-λε-λυ-μην	ἐ-λε-λυ-μεθα
λε-λυ-σαι	λε-λυ-σθε	ἐ-λε-λυ-σο	ἐ-λε-λυ-σθε
λε-λυ-ται	λε-λυ-νται	ἐ-λε-λυ-το	ἐ-λε-λυ-ντο

Participles. All Middle and Passive Participles, **except** Aorist Passive, end in -μενος and are declined like ἀγαθος.

Present, Middle and Passive	λυομενος
Future Middle	λυσομενος
1st Aorist Middle	λυσαμενος
2nd Aorist Middle	γενομενος
Future Passive	λυθησομενος
Perfect, Middle and Passive	λελυμενος

The Aorist Participle Passive is declined as follows:

Singular

	Masc.	Fem.	Neut.
Nom. Voc.	λυθεις	λυθεισα	λυθεν
Acc.	λυθεντα	λυθεισαν	λυθεν
Gen.	λυθεντος	λυθεισης	λυθεντος
Dat.	λυθεντι	λυθειση	λυθεντι

Plural

	Masc.	Fem.	Neut.
Nom. Voc.	λυθεντες	λυθεισαι	λυθεντα
Acc.	λυθεντας	λυθεισας	λυθεντα
Gen.	λυθεντων	λυθεισων	λυθεντων
Dat.	λυθεισι	λυθεισαις	λυθεισι

Infinitives

Present	λυεσθαι
Future Middle	λυσεσθαι
1st Aorist Middle	λυσασθαι
2nd Aorist Middle	γενεσθαι
Future Passive	λυθησεσθαι
1st Aorist Passive	λυθηναι
2nd Aorist Passive	σπαρηναι
Perfect	λελυσθαι

Note:
Principal parts of verbs

You have now learned all the tenses of the regular verb, though there are some additional moods to follow. At the end of the book you will find a chart setting out all the moods and tenses of the verb λυω. This verb, and one or two others, are perfectly regular in the formation of tenses, but the vast majority of Greek verbs form one or other of their tenses in an irregular way. This is regrettable, but cannot now be rectified for the benefit of unfortunate modern students. In order to make it a little easier to identify the various parts of the verb there is a conventional way of listing the " Principal Parts ", which are given as Present Active, Future Active, Aorist Active, Perfect Active, Perfect Passive and Aorist Passive. A list of the main verbs you are likely to need in reading the New Testament is given at the end of the book (pp. 140–4) and you should eventually learn the whole list by heart. This is not so difficult as it may appear, if it is taken piecemeal, say five a day.

From this point it will be assumed that you will look up the verbs which occur in the exercises in order to check the tenses. It would be a good idea to glance through the list now and note a few of the commoner verbs which you have already learnt. In particular, note carefully the last section, which contains a number of defective verbs, in which the tenses are made up of parts from verbs with different stems. These are mostly very common verbs, and a few minutes spent in looking at them now will save a lot of time hunting for them later.

EXERCISE XVIa

ἦν δε ποτε ἀνηρ ὁς ἐπεμφθη ὑπο του βασιλεως εἰς πολιν

ἑτεραν και παρα την ὁδον πορευομενος ἐληφθη ὑπο ληστων.
ὁ ἀνηρ ὀργισθεις εἰπεν, ἐγω εἰμι ὁ του βασιλεως ἀγγελος
και ὑμεις ὑπο του βασιλεως διωχθησεσθε και τιμωρηθησεσθε.
οἱ λησται ἀκουσαντες τουτο ἐφοβηθησαν και διαλεγεσθαι
ἠρξαντο ἀλληλοις. ὁ μεν εἰπεν, ὁ βασιλευς ἐλθων
λημψεται ἡμας και βληθησομεθα εἰς φυλακην. ὁ δε ἀποκριθεις εἰπεν, λυσομεν τον ἀγγελον και φευξομεθα ὡστε μη
ληφθηναι. ὁ δε ἡγεμων εἰπεν, δια τι διαλεγεσθε ἑαυ-
τοις ; ὁ ἀγγελος τεθνηκως οὐ δυνησεται ἀναγγειλαι τον
λογον τῳ βασιλει και νεκρος κεκρυμμενος οὐχ εὑρεθησεται.

διωκω—pursue   τιμωρεω—punish
φοβεω—terrify   διαλεγομαι—discuss
ἀναγγελλω—report   φυλακη—prison
ὡστε (followed by Infinitive expresses consequence)—so that

EXERCISE XVIb

When the disciples came together on the fiftieth day, a
sound was heard as of a strong wind, and the whole house
where they were sitting was filled. And there were seen
tongues as of fire, and they were filled with Holy Spirit,
and began to speak with other tongues. The words were
heard by the people and they were terrified because they
saw the miracle. Then Peter answered and said to them,
" This (τουτο) has happened by the power of God. Jesus
of Nazareth was crucified by you, but was lifted up by
God, and in his name the Holy Spirit has come ".

come together—συν-ερχομαι   fiftieth—πεντηκοστος, -η, -ον
sound—ἠχος, το   as--ὡσπερ
where—οὑ   crucify—σταυροω
lift up—ὑψοω   were seen—ὡφθησαν
strong (of wind)—βιαιος

LESSON XVI

THE VERB—SUBJUNCTIVE MOOD

The Indicative Mood expresses a fact, it *indicates* something.

The Subjunctive Mood expresses a possibility, an uncertainty or an indefinite statement. English sometimes uses " may ", " might ", " would " but does not always clearly indicate the Subjunctive.

The different tenses of the Subjunctive have NO TIME REFERENCE, but differ according to the KIND OF ACTION, just like the Infinitive or Participle, i.e.

The Present Subjunctive refers to a continuous action.

The Aorist Subjunctive refers to a single action.

There is no Future Subjunctive, and the one most commonly used is the Aorist.

Since the Aorist Subjunctive is not a Historic tense it has no augment. It is formed from the Aorist stem, like the Infinitive. The negative of the Subjunctive is $\mu\eta$.

The endings of the Subjunctive are similar to the Indicative but have long vowels, -ω- and -η-, in place of the short Indicative vowels, -o-, -ε- or -a-. The First Aorist Subjunctive is like the Present with the addition of -σ-, the Second Aorist is like the Present, but is from the Aorist stem. The Aorist Passive has Active endings, like the Indicative. The following are the forms:

Active: Present	*1st Aorist*	*2nd Aorist*
λυω	λυσω	βαλω
λυῃς	λυσῃς	βαλῃς
λυῃ	λυσῃ	βαλῃ
λυωμεν	λυσωμεν	βαλωμεν
λυητε	λυσητε	βαλητε
λυωσι(ν)	λυσωσι(ν)	βαλωσι(ν)

74

Middle and Passive

Present	Aorist Middle	Aorist Passive
λυωμαι	λυσωμαι	λυθω
λυη	λυση	λυθης
λυηται	λυσηται	λυθη
λυωμεθα	λυσωμεθα	λυθωμεν
λυησθε	λυσησθε	λυθητε
λυωνται	λυσωνται	λυθωσι (ν)

USES OF THE SUBJUNCTIVE

A. *As Main Verb*

1. *Hortatory*, in First Person only, to express an exhortation.

   Beloved, *let us love* one another: ἀγαπητοι, ἀγαπωμεν ἀλληλους.

   Deliberative, to express a question with a doubt in it. What are we to do? τι ποιησωμεν ;

3. *Prohibition*. Second Person of *Aorist* Subjunctive only.

   Do not do this. μη ποιησης τουτο.

4. *Strong Denial*. οὐ μη with the Aorist Subjunctive is used to express strong denial of a future event.

   He will certainly not escape. οὐ μη καταφυγη.

B. *In Subordinate Clauses*

1. *Final clause*, expressing purpose, introduced by ἱνα or ὁπως.

   He came in order to ask this. ἠλθεν ἱνα τουτο αἰτηση.

2. *Indefinite clause*, introduced by Relative Pronoun or Adverb with ἄν which is equivalent to the English suffix " -ever ".

Whoever believes shall be saved. ὅς ἄν πιστευσῃ σωθησεται.

3. *Temporal clauses* referring to the future and introduced by ἕως ἄν, ἕως οὗ or ἕως ὅτου, all of which mean " until ".

I shall remain until he comes. μενω ἕως ἄν ἔλθῃ.

4. *Conditional clause* referring to the future, introduced by ἐαν which is a combination of εἰ and ἄν (see Lesson XXVII).

5. After verbs of fearing, introduced by μη—" lest ".

He feared lest he should be punished. ἐφοβηθη μη τιμωρηθῃ.

(*Note:* μη here must not be translated as a negative. The sentence in English could equally well be translated " He feared *that* he would be punished ". IN THIS CASE ONLY, the negative of the Subjunctive is οὐ, which follows μη used as a conjunction, e.g. He feared that they would not come—ἐφοβηθη μη αὐτοι οὐκ ἔλθωσι.)

You have now learned enough grammar to be able to begin reading some of the easier parts of the New Testament. It is not possible to do this until you understand the Subjunctive, since it occurs very frequently, and you can hardly read half-a-dozen verses before coming across it.

A good place to start is with the First Epistle of John, which has mostly short sentences and is fairly familiar. There will be some words which you do not understand, but you should be able to guess the meaning from a comparison with the English Bible. It is a good idea to get a modern version, rather than using the somewhat archaic English of the Authorized or Revised, and the best one at present is probably Kingsley Williams, *The New Testament in Plain English.*

The Greek of the New Testament varies quite a lot, and it is best to work through familiar passages first. The Sermon on the Mount is quite simple, and that might be taken after 1 John. Then either a continuation of Matthew, or Mark. The style of Luke and Acts is more classical, and the last part of Acts has a large number of words which do not occur anywhere else in the New Testament. The letters of Paul tend to be very involved in language as well as in thought, but if they are taken slowly they can be sorted out. You can reckon that you know some Greek when you can read and appreciate the Letter to the Hebrews, which contains the most beautiful language in the New Testament. Until you can do that it is better not to look at the book of Revelation, which is very strange Greek indeed, and not the kind to be imitated by a learner.

It is possible, of course, to finish the Grammar first, but it will probably prove more interesting to work through a chapter of the New Testament alternately with the rest of the Lessons. You will meet some words which are unfamiliar, but you can get them by comparison with the English version on your first reading.

EXERCISE XVIIa

ὁ Ἰησους εἰπεν τοις μαθηταις, πορευωμεθα ἀλλαχου εἰς τας ἑτερας κωμας, ἱνα και ἐκει κηρυξω. ὁς ἀν δεχηται με, δεχεται τον πατερα μου. ὁ γαρ υἱος του ἀνθρωπου οὐκ ἠλθεν ἱνα κρινη τον κοσμον, ἀλλ᾽ ἱνα ὁ κοσμος δι᾽ αὐτου σωθη. ὁ δε κοσμος οὐ μη πιστευση εἰς ἐμε ἑως ἀν ἐλθω ἐπι των νεφελων του οὐρανου. οἱ δε μαθηται ἀποκριθεντες

εἶπον, κυριε, τι ποιησωμεν ; ἐαν οἱ ὀχλοι τους λογους σου
μη ἀκουσωσι, πως τους ἡμετερους ἀκουσουσι ; ὁ δε Ἰησους
εἶπεν, ὁπου ἀν κηρυξητε το εὐαγγελιον, μη φοβηθητε μη
οἱ ἀνθρωποι ἀποκτεινωσιν ὑμας, ἐγω γαρ μεθ'ὑμων εἰμι εἰς
τον αἰωνα.

ἀλλαχου—elsewhere	κωμη—village
ἀποκτεινω—kill	νεφελη—cloud
ὁπου—where	κηρυσσω—preach
ὀχλος—crowd	πως—how
ἐκει—there	

EXERCISE XVIIb

Paul wrote in his letter, " What shall we do then? Shall
we continue in sin, that grace may abound?" But whoever sees the love of God is not able to sin, and whoever
sins will never enter the kingdom of heaven. Jesus came
in order that we might have life, and in order that we might
help one another. Let us keep his commandments until we
see him in his glory. Our hope is in him so that we do
not fear that he will desert us. Whenever we enter into
temptation we can say to him, " Lord, do not turn away
from thy people ".

abound—περισσευω	desert, abandon—καταλειπω
temptation—πειρασμος	turn away—ἀποστρεφω
letter—ἐπιστολη	whenever—ὁταν

LESSON XVII

CONTRACTED VERBS

We have already met a few verbs which have stems ending in a vowel, a, ε, or o, and for the most part we have avoided the Present and Imperfect tenses of these verbs. Since the endings of the Present and Imperfect begin with a vowel it means that two vowels come together, and it is a case of love at first sight, resulting in immediate marriage! The technical term for this marriage is " crasis ", or " mixing ", and the rules are quite simple. Just as in any other marriage there are two possibilities—either one partner is so strong that it dominates the other, or the two partners influence one another and the result is a harmonious combination. We may refer to the stem vowel as the husband since that is usually the dominant partner, but sometimes the wife manages to avoid being completely suppressed and pushes in an unobtrusive iota subscript without her husband realizing it.

The a verbs are most masculine when they meet ε or η, and here they completely dominate (except for the iota subscript). When they meet o or ω they become henpecked!

a with ε or η—a	a with $\varepsilon\iota$ or η—α
a with o, ov or ω—ω	a with $o\iota$—ω

The ε verbs are almost entirely under the wife's thumb except when they meet ε or o.

ε with ε—$\varepsilon\iota$	ε with o—ov

ε with long vowel or diphthong disappears.

The o verbs are the most masterful and always dominate the ending, but an iota makes them shout $o\iota$!

o with short vowel—ου   o with long vowel—ω
o with any combination of ι (including subscript)—οι

(*Note:* The Present Infinitive Active ending -ειν is already a contraction of ε + εν and the stem vowels α and ο are added to this, so that α + ε + ε = α and ο + ε + ε = ου. There is therefore no ι involved.)

From these rules the tenses can easily be worked out as they are tabulated below.

Active

Present Indicative

τιμω	φιλω	δουλω
τιμας	φιλεις	δουλοις
τιμα	φιλει	δουλοι
τιμωμεν	φιλουμεν	δουλουμεν
τιματε	φιλειτε	δουλουτε
τιμωσι(ν)	φιλουσι(ν)	δουλουσι(ν)

Imperfect Indicative

ἐτιμων	ἐφιλουν	ἐδουλουν
ἐτιμας	ἐφιλεις	ἐδουλους
ἐτιμα	ἐφιλει	ἐδουλου
ἐτιμωμεν	ἐφιλουμεν	ἐδουλουμεν
ἐτιματε	ἐφιλειτε	ἐδουλουτε
ἐτιμων	ἐφιλουν	ἐδουλουν

Present Subjunctive

τιμω	φιλω	δουλω
τιμας	φιλης	δουλοις
τιμα	φιλη	δουλοι
τιμωμεν	φιλωμεν	δουλωμεν
τιματε	φιλητε	δουλωτε
τιμωσι(ν)	φιλωσι(ν)	δουλωσι(ν)

Present Infinitive

τιμαν   φιλειν   δουλουν

Present Participle

τιμων   φιλων   δουλων
τιμωσα   φιλουσα   δουλουσα
τιμων   φιλουν   δουλουν

Middle and Passive

Present Indicative

τιμωμαι   φιλουμαι   δουλουμαι
τιμᾳ   φιλει, φιλῃ   δουλοι
τιμαται   φιλειται   δουλουται
τιμωμεθα   φιλουμεθα   δουλουμεθα
τιμασθε   φιλεισθε   δουλουσθε
τιμωνται   φιλουνται   δουλουνται

Imperfect Indicative

ἐτιμωμην   ἐφιλουμην   ἐδουλουμην
ἐτιμω   ἐφιλου   ἐδουλου
ἐτιματο   ἐφιλειτο   ἐδουλουτο
ἐτιμωμεθα   ἐφιλουμεθα   ἐδουλουμεθα
ἐτιμασθε   ἐφιλεισθε   ἐδουλουσθε
ἐτιμωντο   ἐφιλουντο   ἐδουλουντο

Present Subjunctive

τιμωμαι   φιλωμαι   δουλωμαι
τιμᾳ   φιλῃ   δουλοι
τιμαται   φιληται   δουλωται
τιμωμεθα   φιλωμεθα   δουλωμεθα
τιμασθε   φιλησθε   δουλωσθε
τιμωνται   φιλωνται   δουλωνται

Present Infinitive

τιμασθαι   φιλεισθαι   δουλουσθαι

Present Participle

τιμωμενος   φιλουμενος   δουλουμενος
τιμωμενη   φιλουμενη   δουλουμενη
τιμωμενον   φιλουμενον   δουλουμενον

EXERCISE XVIIIa

ἐν τῳ κοσμῳ δηλον ἐστιν ὅτι εἰ τις (anyone) βοᾳ, τιμαται· ἀλλ᾽ εἰ τις ταπεινουται ἡ δοξα αὐτου οὐ φανερουται. ἰατρος τις τους πτωχους θεραπευει καὶ ἰαται, ἀλλ᾽οὐδεις φιλει αὐτον. εἰ δε ζητει την δοξαν των ἀνθρωπων καὶ την ἑαυτου σοφιαν ὑψοι, παντες (all) τιμωσιν αὐτον καὶ ὁ οἰκος αὐτου πεπληρωμενος ἐστι. οὐ θεωρειτε ὅτι οἱ πολλους (many) λογους λαλουντες σοφοι ἐπικαλουνται ; ἀγαλλιωμεθα οὖν καὶ χαρας πληρωμεθα ὅτι ἐν τοις οὐρανοις οἱ ταπεινωθεντες ὑψωθησονται, καὶ οἱ ἑαυτους ὑψωσαντες ταπεινωθησονται. ὁ ἀνθρωπος οὐ τῃ ἑαυτου σοφιᾳ δικαιουται ἀλλα τῃ του Θεου ἀγαπῃ. το εὐαγγελιον μαρτυρει ὅτι ὁ Ἰησους ἐσταυρωθη ἱνα οἱ ἀνθρωποι δικαιωθωσι, καὶ ἱνα ἐν τῃ ἐσχατῃ ἡμερᾳ σωσῃ τους ἀγαπωντας αὐτον.

EXERCISE XVIIIb

Jesus said, " If you love me you will keep my commandments." But if we look at the world we see that men do not do this. They desire salvation, but they are not willing to humble themselves. They are filled with wickedness and worship idols (εἰδωλα). Let us ask, " Who (τις ;) is justified by his works? " The Scriptures witness that no one is righteous. Man must be silent when God speaks in order to manifest his truth. When he is born into the world he allows sin to take hold of him, and he loves his own glory, and exalts himself. Let us ask God to heal our sin and to manifest his glory in us, that we may rejoice greatly in the day of the Lord.

βοαω—shout
τιμαω—honour
ἀγαπαω—love
σιωπαω—be silent
ἐαω—allow
ἰαομαι—heal
ἀγαλλιαομαι—rejoice
  greatly
γενναομαι—be born
πτωχος—poor
ὁραω—see
φιλεω—love
ζητεω—seek
θεωρεω—look at
λαλεω—speak
ἐπικαλεω—surname
ἑαυτου—(see p. 116)

τηρεω—watch, keep
ἐπιθυμεω—desire (+ genit.)
μαρτυρεω—witness
αἰτεω—ask
τις ; (question)—who?
ταπεινοω—humble
φανεροω—manifest
ὑψοω—lift up, exalt
πληροω—fill
δικαιοω—justify
σταυροω—crucify
οὐδεις—no one
λατρευω—worship
τις (statement)—someone,
  any one
δηλος—clear

THE -μι VERBS

Most of the verbs in the New Testament are of the form you have already learnt, ending in -ω, but these are not quite the only verbs, nor are they of the oldest type. Originally the verb was probably formed from two sounds, one indicating an action, and the other indicating the person acting. The earliest ending was probably the personal pronoun in the forms -μαι (me), -σαι (you), -ται (that), which we find surviving in the passive, but these were also modified to -μι, -σι, -τι, in order to provide a separate form for the active. Later more endings were used to differentiate different shades of meaning, and these early endings tended to drop out, so that the later the Greek, the less common they become. There are, however, three verbs in the New Testament which have retained them, and a few others which have some fragments.

All these words except εἰμι (I am) are transitive, and have very fundamental meanings—I put, give, set or stand—so that although they are few they occur very frequently. The three chief are:

τιθημι—prevailing vowel ε—stem θε—I place
διδωμι—   ,,   ,, ο— ,,   δο—I give
ἱστημι—   ,,   ,, α— ,,   στα—I make to stand

In the Present stem there is Reduplication with the modifications of θ to τ in τιθημι and σ to a rough breathing in ἱστημι, and also the singular has a lengthened stem vowel.

Since these three are very similar, apart from the stem vowels, it is convenient to look at them side by side, in

the different tenses.   Tenses enclosed in brackets are not
found in the New Testament.

Present Indicative Active

τίθημι	δίδωμι	ἵστημι
τίθης	δίδως	ἵστης
τίθησι(ν)	δίδωσι(ν)	ἵστησι(ν)
τίθεμεν	δίδομεν	ἵσταμεν
τίθετε	δίδοτε	ἵστατε
τιθέασι(ν)	διδόασι(ν)	ἱστᾶσι(ν)

(*Note:* The third person plural of τίθημι and δίδωμι is
never contracted.)

Imperfect Indicative Active

ἐτίθην	ἐδίδουν	[ἵστην]
ἐτίθεις	ἐδίδους	[ἵστης]
ἐτίθει	ἐδίδου	[ἵστη]
ἐτίθεμεν	ἐδίδομεν	[ἵσταμεν]
ἐτίθετε	ἐδίδοτε	[ἵστατε]
ἐτίθεσαν, ἐτίθουν	ἐδίδοσαν, ἐδίδουν	[ἵστασαν]

Present and Imperfect Indicative Middle and Passive

τίθεμαι	[ἐτιθέμην]	δίδομαι	ἐδιδόμην
τίθεσαι	[ἐτίθεσο]	δίδοσαι	ἐδίδοσο
τίθεται	[ἐτίθετο]	δίδοται	ἐδίδοτο
τιθέμεθα	[ἐτιθέμεθα]	διδόμεθα	ἐδιδόμεθα
τίθεσθε	[ἐτίθεσθε]	δίδοσθε	ἐδίδοσθε
τίθενται	[ἐτίθεντο]	δίδονται	ἐδίδοντο
	ἵσταμαι	[ἱστάμην]	
	ἵστασαι	[ἵστασο]	
	ἵσταται	[ἵστατο]	
	ἱστάμεθα	[ἱστάμεθα]	
	ἵστασθε	[ἵστασθε]	
	ἵστανται	[ἵσταντο]	

Infinitives and Participles

Active

τιθεναι τιθεις	διδοναι διδους	ἱσταναι ἱστας
τιθεισα	διδουσα	ἱστασα
τιθεν	διδον	ἱσταν
(see p. 71)	(see p. 58)	(see p. 59)

Middle and Passive

τιθεσθαι τιθεμενος	διδοσθαι διδομενος	ἱστασθαι ἱσταμενος
τιθεμενη	διδομενη	ἱσταμενη
τιθεμενον	διδομενον	ἱσταμενον

Aorist Indicative Active

(*Note:* κ in place of the usual σ.)

Singular	Plural	Singular	Plural
ἐθηκα	ἐθηκαμεν	ἐδωκα	ἐδωκαμεν
ἐθηκας	ἐθηκατε	ἐδωκας	ἐδωκατε
ἐθηκε	ἐθηκαν	ἐδωκε	ἐδωκαν

ἱστημι has two Aorists, which differ in meaning, the First Aorist being Transitive and meaning " I caused to stand ", and the Second Aorist being Intransitive and meaning " I stood ". The First Aorist is quite regular in form, the Second has forms like the Aorist Passive.

1st Aorist	2nd Aorist
ἐστησα	ἐστην
ἐστησας	ἐστης
ἐστησε	ἐστη
ἐστησαμεν	ἐστημεν
ἐστησατε	ἐστητε
ἐστησαν	ἐστησαν

(*Note:* The third person plural is the same in each form, and its meaning must be inferred from the context. It causes no confusion, since if it has an object it is First Aorist and if not, it is Second.)

Aorist Indicative Middle (Second Aorist)

ἐθεμην	ἐθεμεθα	ἐδομην	ἐδομεθα
ἐθου	ἐθεσθε	ἐδου	ἐδοσθε
ἐθετο	ἐθεντο	ἐδοτο	ἐδοντο

Aorist Infinitives
  Active

		1st	2nd
θειναι	δουναι	στησαι	στηναι

  Middle

θεσθαι	δοσθαι

Aorist Participles
  Active

θεις	δους	στησας	στας
θεισα	δουσα	στησασα	στασα
θεν	δον	στησαν	σταν

  Middle

θεμενος-η-ον	δομενος-η-ον

Subjunctives

The Present and Aorist Subjunctives of τιθημι and ἱστημι are quite regular. The Present and Aorist Subunctives Active and Middle (but NOT Passive) of διδωμι have ω instead of η in all parts.

διδω	δω	διδωμαι	δωμαι
διδως	δως	διδω	δω
διδω	δω [δωη]	διδωται	δωται
διδωμεν	δωμεν	διδωμεθα	δωμεθα
διδωτε	δωτε	διδωσθε	δωσθε
διδωσι	δωσι	διδωνται	δωνται

OTHER TENSES are regularly conjugated as follows:

Active

Future	θησω	δωσω	στησω—I shall cause to stand
Perfect	τεθεικα	δεδωκα	*έστηκα —I stand

Middle

Future	θησομαι	δωσομαι	στησομαι —I shall stand

M. and P.

Perfect	τεθειμαι	δεδομαι	

Passive

Future	τεθησομαι	δοθησομαι	σταθησομαι—I shall stand
Aorist	ἐτεθην	ἐδοθην	ἐσταθην—I stood

(*Note* the meanings of the tenses of ἱστημι as given on the right. The Present, Imperfect, Future and First Aorist Active are all Transitive; the rest are Intransitive.

* Perfect Infinitive is ἑσταναι and there are two forms of Participle—ἑστως, ἑστωσα, ἑστως and ἑστηκως, ἑστηκυια, ἑστηκος.)

OTHER VERBS IN -μι (FRAGMENTS)

φημι (I say), has Pres. Indic. Act.—φημι   φης   φησι
                                       φαμεν   φατε   φασι
and Imperf. Indic. Act. 3rd sing.—ἐφη 3rd plur.—ἐφησαν
ἀφιημι (let go, forgive)

The root of ἱημι is ἑ, but the simple verb is not found in the New Testament, and many parts are assimilated to -ω verbs. The following must be noted:

Pres. Indic. Act.	3rd sing. Imperf. Indic. Act.—*ἤφιε*
ἀφιημι	Pres. Infin. Act.—*ἀφιεναι*
ἀφιης, ἀφεις	3rd plur. Pres. Indic. Pass.—*ἀφιενται*
ἀφιησι	„ „ Perf. „ „ —*ἀφεωνται*
ἀφιεμεν, ἀφιομεν	2nd Aor. Subj. Act.—*ἀφω, ἀφης, ἀφη*
ἀφιετε	*ἀφωμεν, ἀφητε, ἀφωσι*
ἀφιασι, ἀφιουσι	„ „ Part. Act.—*ἀφεις, ἀφεισα, ἀφεν*

„   „   Imper.„   2nd sing.—*ἀφες*
„   „   „   „   „   plur.—*ἀφετε*

Fut. Indic. Act.—*ἀφησω*   1st Aor. Indic. Act.—*ἀφηκα*
„   „   Pass.—*ἀφεθησομαι* „   „,   „   Pass.—*ἀφεθην*

συν-ιημι (I understand) has the following forms:

Pres. Indic. Act. 2nd plur.—*συνιετε*
„   „   „   3rd plur.—*συνιασι*
Fut. Indic. Act. 3rd plur.—*συνησουσι*
1st Aor. Indic. Act. 2nd plur.—*συνηκατε*
„   „   „   „   3rd plur.—*συνηκαν*
Pres. Imper. Act. 3rd sing.—*συνιετω*
2nd Aor. Imper. Act. 2nd plur.—*συνετε*
Pres. Infin. Act.—*συνιεναι*
„   Part.   „   —*συνιων* and *συνιεις* (genitive—
συνιεντος)
2nd Aor. Subj. Act. 2nd plur.—*συνητε*
„   „   „   „   3rd plur.—*συνωσι*

THE DEFECTIVE VERB *οἶδα*

This is a Perfect tense used as a Present. It comes
from the very old Sanskrit root vid- which is connected
with the Latin " vision " and allied words. The Present
is not found, but the Aorist is *εἶδυν* (I saw) and the
Perfect, *οἶδα*, means " I have seen ", therefore I KNOW.

Perfect Indic.	*Pluperf. Indic.*	*Subjunctive*	*Infinitive*
(I know)	(I knew)		εἰδεναι
οἰδα	ἠδειν	εἰδω	
οἰδας	ἠδεις	εἰδης	*Participle*
οἰδε	ἠδει	εἰδη	εἰδως
οἰδαμεν	ἠδειμεν	εἰδωμεν	εἰδυια
οἰδατε, ἰστε	ἠδειτε	εἰδητε	εἰδος
οἰδασι, ἰσασι	ἠδεισαν, ἠδεσαν	εἰδωσι	

EXERCISE XIXa

οἰκοδεσποτης τις ἐβουλετο ἀπελθειν εἰς ἑτεραν πολιν και στησας τους δουλους ἐνωπιον αὐτου ἐδωκεν αὐτοις ἀργυρια, ἱνα ἐργασωνται ἑως ἀν ἐλθῃ. οἱ δουλοι σταντες ἐλεγον προς ἀλληλους, τι ποιησωμεν ; ὁ μεν εἰπεν, ἀγορασωμεν προβατα, ἱνα τους ἀμνους ἀποδομενοι ἀργυρια λαβωμεν. ὁ δε παραστας εἰπεν, ἐγω δε θησω τα ἀργυρια εἰς την τραπεζαν ἱνα μη ἀπολεσω αὐτα. ὁ οἰκοδεσποτης ἐλθων εἰπεν αὐτοις λογον ἀποδουναι. ὁ μεν ἐλαβε πεντε ἀργυρια και παρεθηκε τῳ δεσποτῃ δεκα · ὁ δε δεσποτης εἰπεν, καλως ἐποιησας, καταστησω σε ἀρχοντα του οἰκου. ὁ δε ἐλαβε δυο ἀργυρια και ἀπεδωκε τα δυο, και ὁ δεσποτης ὀργισθεις εἰπεν, οἰδα σε κακον δουλον ὀντα, και παρεδωκε τοις ὑπηρεταις ἱνα εἰς φυλακην βληθῃ.

παριστημι—(intrans.) stand beside, (trans.) set beside
παρατιθημι—set by the side of
παραδιδωμι—hand over
καθιστημι—set over
ἀγοραζω—buy
ἀποδιδωμι—repay; Mid.—sell
ἀπολεσω, aorist subjunctive of ἀπολλυω—lose
ἐνωπιον—in front of
ἀποδιδωμι λογον—give account
τραπεζα—table used by money-changers, hence the ancient " bank "
ἀμνος—lamb
τις—indefinite pronoun, here translate " a "
οἰκοδεσποτης—householder
ὑπηρετης—officer

EXERCISE XIXb

The Lord said, " Whosoever has, to him shall be given ". If we wish to receive his grace we ought to give him our love. He has set us in the world so that we may do his work, and if we do his will he will raise us up at the last day. He knows that we are sinners, but he will forgive our sins and set us before his Father as holy. Let us give to him our love that we may know his will and do it. Not as Judas betrayed him to the High Priests, and sold his Master, but as the martyrs laid down their lives for him. Let us take the armour of God that we may stand in the evil day, and not be separated from him.

raise up—ἀνιστημι
set before—παριστημι
sell—ἀποδιδομαι
separate—ἀφιστημι
as—καθως
lay down one's life—τιθημι
   την ψυχην

forgive—ἀφιημι
betray—προδιδωμι
armour—πανοπλιον
high priest—ἀρχιερευς
for, on behalf of—ὑπερ with genitive
martyr—μαρτυς -υρος (m.)

LESSON XIX

THE IMPERATIVE MOOD

Turn to Matthew viii. 9, and read what the centurion says to his servants. All his words are commands, and they are expressed by the Imperative (" commanding ") mood. The centurion uses three different tenses out of the five which you need to learn.

There are two Imperatives in each Voice, Present and Aorist, but the Present has the same form in Middle and Passive, which makes five.

The distinction is the same as that in the Subjunctive, the Present referring to continual or repeated action and the Aorist to simple action, though the New Testament is not always very precise. But it is important to note that the difference is *never* of time; you can only order someone to do something in the future. Also strictly speaking the Imperative has only one person, because an order is always addressed to " you ", but Greek also allows (with Indian languages) the possibility of a third person imperative when an indirect order is given. This is one of the few places where English is more logical, and says " let him do this " or " let them do this ".

The regular Imperative forms are as shown on pages 94 and 95.

The following irregular Imperatives should be noted:

εἰμι—ἴσθι, ἔστω, ἔστε, ἔστωσαν. οἶδα—ἴσθι, ἴστε. φημι— φαθι, φατε. εἰδον—ἴδε, ἴδετε. εἰπον—εἴπε, εἴπετε. ἔσχον— σχες, σχετε. ἰδου is often found as an exclamation, "Look!"

The Second Aorist Passive is in *-ηθι* instead of *-ητι—*
σπαρηθι, σταληθι.

EXERCISE XXa

νυν ἐντολας δωσω, ὑμεις αὐτας τηρειτε.
μαθηται, στητε—καθιζετε.
πρωτε μαθητα, το βιβλιον δος ἐμοι—λαβε.
δευτερε μαθητα, το ὀνομα σου γραψον.
τριτε μαθητα, την χειρα σου ὑψωσον—ἐπι της τραπεζης θες.
τεταρτε και πεμπτε μαθηται, ἐξελθετε ἀπο του οἰκου.
ἑκτε μαθητα, ἀναγαγε αὐτους εἰς τον οἰκον.
ἑβδομε μαθητα, εἰπε αὐτοις καθισαι.
ὀγδοε μαθητα, του προσωπου σου ἁπτου.
ἐνατε μαθητα, μη καθιζε, στηθι.
δεκατε μαθητα, εἰπε αὐτῳ καθισαι.

Note: This exercise not only gives practice in the Imperative, but also gives the first ten *Ordinal* numerals in
the Vocative Case. Ordinal numerals give the order in
which something comes, i.e. first, second, third, etc., and
they are declined like the first and second declension adjectives. δευτερος has ρ as the last letter of the stem and
so the feminine is in *-α*; all the rest have feminine in *-η*.

The last but one sentence is a negative command, or
prohibition. When the prohibition is to stop doing something already begun the construction used is μη with the
Present Imperative, as here. When the prohibition is
against doing something not already begun the construction is μη with the Aorist Subjunctive.

E.g. Stop saying—μη λεγε.

Do not say (when it is not already begun)—μη εἰπης.

	S/P		ACTIVE Pres. & 2nd Aor.	1st Aor.	M. & P. Pres. & 2nd Aor.	MIDDLE 1st Aor.	PASSIVE 1st Aor.
λυω	S	2	λυε	λυσον	λυου	λυσαι	λυθητι
		3	λυετω	λυσατω	λυεσθω	λυσασθω	λυθητω
	P	2	λυετε	λυσατε	λυεσθε	λυσασθε	λυθητε
		3	λυετωσαν	λυσατωσαν	λυεσθωσαν	λυσασθωσαν	λυθητωσαν
τιμαω	S	2	τιμα	τιμησον	τιμω	τιμησαι	τιμηθητι
		3	τιματω	τιμησατω	τιμασθω	τιμησασθω	τιμηθητω
	P	2	τιματε	τιμησατε	τιμασθε	τιμησασθε	τιμηθητε
		3	τιματωσαν	τιμησατωσαν	τιμασθωσαν	τιμησασθωσαν	τιμηθητωσαν
φιλεω	S	2	φιλει	φιλησον	φιλου	φιλησαι	φιληθητι
		3	φιλειτω	φιλησατω	φιλεισθω	φιλησασθω	φιληθητω
	P	2	φιλειτε	φιλησατε	φιλεισθε	φιλησασθε	φιληθητε
		3	φιλειτωσαν	φιλησατωσαν	φιλεισθωσαν	φιλησασθωσαν	φιληθητωσαν
δουλοω	S	2	δουλου	δουλωσον	δουλου	δουλωσαι	δουλωθητι
		3	δουλουτω	δουλωσατω	δουλουσθω	δουλωσασθω	δουλωθητω
	P	2	δουλουτε	δουλωσατε	δουλουσθε	δουλωσασθε	δουλωθητε

				2nd Aor.		2nd Aor.
τίθημι	S	2	τίθει	θές	θοῦ	τεθῆτι
		3	τιθέτω	θέτω	θέσθω	τεθήτω
	P	2	τίθετε	θέτε	θέσθε	τεθῆτε
		3	τιθέτωσαν	θέτωσαν	θέσθωσαν	τεθήτωσαν
δίδωμι	S	2	δίδου	δός	δοῦ	δοθῆτι
		3	διδότω	δότω	δόσθω	δοθήτω
	P	2	δίδοτε	δότε	δόσθε	δοθῆτε
		3	διδότωσαν	δότωσαν	δόσθωσαν	δοθήτωσαν
				1st Aor. Act. / **2nd Aor. Act.**		
ἵστημι	S	2	ἵστη	στῆσον / στῆθι		σταθῆτι
		3	ἱστάτω	στησάτω / στήτω		σταθήτω
	P	2	ἵστατε	στήσατε / στῆτε		σταθῆτε
		3	ἱστάτωσαν	στησάτωσαν / στήτωσαν		σταθήτωσαν

Note: Present Imperative of ἵστημι is not actually found in N.T.

95

EXERCISE XXb

Rules for Students

Get up early in the morning.
Wash yourselves with water.
Do not stay in bed for a long time.
Listen to the teacher and do not go to sleep in the class.
Write down the wise words of the teacher.
Answer the questions of the teacher quickly.
Read the books, and keep their words in your heart.
Do not cease to pray.

Notes:

1. early in the morning—πρωΐ.
2. wash—λουω (see Lesson XIV).
3. bed—κλινη. for a long time—μακρον χρονον (Accusative of duration).
4. go to sleep—κοιμαομαι (Passive—use Aorist Subjunctive). class—σχολη from which we get " school ".
6. quickly—ταχεως (see Lesson XXI). question—ἐρωτημα, -ατος, το.
8. cease—(see Lesson XIV). pray—εὐχομαι.

A very good example of the difference between the Present and Aorist Imperatives is seen in the two versions of the Lord's Prayer in Matthew vi. 11, where " give us this day " refers to a single action, and Luke xi. 3 where " give us day by day " refers to a repeated action. In the first case the Imperative is Aorist, and in the second it is Present.

ADJECTIVES

You have had a number of adjectives already, all of which had the same type of endings, with masculine and neuter of the second declension, and feminine of the first. There are a few more types in Greek, but only the following need be noted specially:

Type 1. Some words have only two terminations, the masculine and feminine being identical, e.g. αἰωνιος and words beginning with α-privative, e.g. ἀδυνατος, ἄθεος, ἀθεσμος.

Type 2. The two following are irregular in masculine and neuter nominative and accusative singular:

μεγας—great

Singular

Nom. Voc.	μεγας	μεγαλη	μεγα
Acc.	μεγαν	μεγαλην	μεγα
Gen.	μεγαλου	μεγαλης	μεγαλου
Dat.	μεγαλῳ	μεγαλῃ	μεγαλῳ

Plural

Nom. Voc.	μεγαλοι	μεγαλαι	μεγαλα
Acc.	μεγαλους	μεγαλας	μεγαλα
Den.	μεγαλων	μεγαλων	μεγαλων
Gat.	μεγαλοις	μεγαλαις	μεγαλοις

πολυς—much (plural—many)

Singular

Nom. Voc.	πολυς	πολλη	πολυ
Acc.	πολυν	πολλην	πολυ
Gen.	πολλου	πολλης	πολλου
Dat.	πολλῳ	πολλη	πολλῳ

Plural

Nom. Voc.	πολλοι	πολλαι	πολλα
Acc.	πολλους	πολλας	πολλα
Gen.	πολλων	πολλων	πολλων
Dat.	πολλοις	πολλαις	πολλοις

Type 3. Two termination adjectives with third declension consonant endings:

| | Singular | | Plural | |
	M.F.	N.	M.F.	N.
Nom.	ἀφρων (foolish)	ἀφρον	ἀφρονες	ἀφρονα
Voc.	ἀφρον	ἀφρον	ἀφρονες	ἀφρονα
Acc.	ἀφρονα	ἀφρον	ἀφρονας	ἀφρονα
Gen.	ἀφρονος		ἀφρονων	
Dat.	ἀφρονι		ἀφροσι	

Type 4. Two termination adjectives with third declension vowel endings:

| | Singular | | Plural | |
	M.F.	N.	M.F.	N.
Nom.	ἀληθης	ἀληθες	ἀληθεις	ἀληθη
Voc.	ἀληθες	ἀληθες	ἀληθεις	ἀληθη
Acc.	ἀληθη	ἀληθες	ἀληθεις	ἀληθη
Gen.	ἀληθους		ἀληθων	
Dat.	ἀληθει		ἀληθεσι	

Type 5. The irregular adjective πας—all, every:

Singular

Nom. Voc.	πας	πασα	παν
Acc.	παντα	πασαν	παν
Gen.	παντος	πασης	παντος
Dat.	παντι	παση	παντι

Plural

Nom. Voc.	παντες	πασαι	παντα
Acc.	παντας	πασας	παντα
Gen.	παντων	πασων	παντων
Dat.	πασι	πασαις	πασι

(*Note:* Where πας means "all", it indicates a definite number, therefore the noun always has an article.

Participles are also adjectives (see Lesson XII).)

The following are examples from Greek poets:

1. των εὐτυχουντων παντες εἰσι συγγενεις.
2. ὁ γραμματων ἀπειρος οὐ βλεπει βλεπων.
3. και πολλ᾿ ἀπ᾿ ἐχθρων μανθανουσιν οἱ σοφοι.
4. φθειρουσιν ἠθη χρησθ᾿ὁμιλιαι κακαι.
5. θεου θελοντος, δυνατα παντα γιγνεται (a variant form of γινεται).
6. ἐνεστι γαρ πως τουτο τη τυραννιδι νοσημα, τοις φιλοισι* μη πεποιθεναι (to trust).
7. το σωμα θνητον, ἡ δε ψυχη ἀθανατος.

εὐτυχεω—prosper	χρηστος—excellent
ὁμιλια—relationship	θνητος—mortal
νοσημα—disease	ἐχθρος—enemy
ἠθος -ους, το—custom, manners	ἀπειρος—unskilled
	πως—somehow
συγγενης—akin	ἀθανατος—immortal

(*Note:* * In poetry the dative plural sometimes has an ι added to help the metre.)

EXERCISE XXIa

παντες λεγουσιν ὁτι δει τον ἀνθρωπον το ἀγαθον ποιειν, ἀλλα παντες οὐ ποιουσι. ὁ μεν λογος αὐτων ἀληθης, τα δε ἐργα ψευδη. ἀνθρωπος γαρ ἀφρων ἐστι και πληρης πασης ἀδικιας. καιπερ θελων το ἀγαθον ποιησαι, το κακον πρασσει, και το θελημα αὐτου ἀσθενες ὑπαρχει. οἱ φιλουντες το ἀληθες φιλουσι μεγα τι, ἀλλα ἀδυνατον ἐστιν ἀει το ἀληθες εἰπειν.

ἀληθης—true
πληρης—full
ἀφρων—foolish
ὑπαρχει—is, exists
ἀδυνατος—impossible
πρασσω—do, practise

ψευδης—false
ἀσθενης—weak
καιπερ—although
τι—something
ἀει—always

EXERCISE XXIb

Love is great and good, and those who seek love will find the true joy. The foolish men are full of wickedness, and do not seek good things. They all tell lies, and their works are all evil. If a man wishes to speak true things and to do good he finds much joy. But men are weak, and unskilled in (of) righteousness. Many men wish to do great things in the world, and to gain eternal life, but they are deceived. It is impossible for a weak man to do the truth, but by the grace of God all things are possible.

deceive—πλαναω   possible—δυνατος

LESSON XXI

COMPARISON OF ADJECTIVES, ADVERBS

There are two ways of forming comparatives in Greek, as in English:

1. By using " more "—μαλλον and " most "—μαλιστα.
2. By adding suffixes " -er "—τερος and " -est "—τατος.

There are also two ways of expressing the object with which the comparison is made:

1. By using " than "—ἠ and the same case.
2. By using the Comparative Genitive.

1. The regular method of forming comparatives and superlatives is by adding -τερος and -τατος to the stem. If the previous vowel is short the stem-vowel is lengthened, e.g.

	Positive	*Comparative*	*Superlative*
(strong)	ἰσχυρος	ἰσχυροτερος	[ἰσχυροτατος]
(wise)	σοφος	σοφωτερος	[σοφωτατος]
(careful)	ἀκριβης	[ἀκριβεστερος]	ἀκριβεστατος
(religious)	δεισιδαιμων	δεισιδαιμονεσ-τερος	[δεισιδαιμο-νεστατος]

BUT the regular superlative occurs only rarely in the New Testament and in other places the comparative is used with a superlative meaning. None of the forms in brackets occurs in the N.T.

2. The following irregular comparisons are important and MUST BE LEARNT:

ἀγαθος—good   κρεισσων, κρειττων—   κρατιστος—best
                 better

κακος—bad   χειρων, ἡσσων, ἡττων—worse

πολυς—much   πλειων, πλεων—more   πλειστος—most

μικρος—little   μικροτερος, ἐλασσων, ἐλαττων—less   ἐλαχιστος—least

μεγας—great   μειζων—greater   μεγιστος—greatest

κρατιστος only in the title κρατιστε—" your Excellency ".

(*Note.* Most of these are irregular also in English.)

The declension of the irregular comparatives in -ων is as follows:

Singular

	M.F.	N.
Nom.	μειζων	μειζον
Acc.	μειζονα, μειζω	μειζον
Gen.	μειζονος	μειζονος
Dat.	μειζονι	μειζονι

Plural

	M.F.	N.
Nom.	μειζονες, μειζους	μειζονα, μειζω
Acc.	μειζονας, μειζους	μειζονα, μειζω
Gen.	μειζονων	μειζονων
Dat.	μειζοσι	μειζοσι

ADVERBS

Adverbs answer one of the questions " how ", " why ", " when ", " where ". Some of them exist alone, whilst others are formed from adjectives, just as they are formed in English by adding " -ly " to adjectives. In Greek they are formed by changing the -ν of the genitive plural to -ς, e.g. true—ἀληθων, truly—ἀληθως; wise—σοφων, wisely—σοφως. The regular comparative adverb ends in -τερον and the superlative in -τατα, but the latter is not found in the New Testament.

The following adverbs are irregular and MUST BE LEARNT:

εὐ— well	βελτιον, κρεισσον— better	[βελτιστα]— best
καλως— well, finely	καλλιον— more finely	[καλλιστα]— most finely
κακως— badly	ἡσσον, ἡττον— worse	[ἡκιστα]— worst
[μαλα]— much	μαλλον— more	μαλιστα— most
πολυ— much	πλειον, πλεον— more	[πλειστα]— most
ἐγγυς— near	ἐγγυτερον— nearer	ἐγγιστα— nearest
ταχυ, ταχεως— quickly	ταχιον— more quickly	ταχιστα— most quickly

(*Note:* The neuter accusative (singular or plural) is often used as an adverb, e.g. only—μονον, much—πολυ or πολλα.
ὡς with a superlative expresses " as —— as possible ", e.g. ὡς ταχιστα—as quickly as possible.)

EXERCISE XXIIa

Some lines from Greek authors:

1. κρεισσον σιωπαν ἐστιν ἡ λαλειν ματην.
2. οὐδεις ἀναγκης μαλλον ἰσχυει νομος.
3. αἱ δευτεραι πως φροντιδες σοφωτεραι.

4. ὁ πλειστα πρασσων πλεισθ'* ἁμαρτανει βροτων.
5. ἐστιν ὁ μεν χειρων, ὁ δε ἀμεινων προς ἐργον ἑκαστον
   οὐδεις δ' ἀνθρωπων αὐτος προς ἁπαντα σοφος.
6. χρησμος 'Απολλωνος ἠν ἐν Δελφοις ·
   σοφος Σοφοκλης, σοφωτερος Εὐριπιδης,
   ἀνδρων δε παντων Σωκρατης σοφωτατος.
7. πλεον ἡμισυ παντος, ὡς 'Ησιοδος λεγει.
8. ἀριστον ὑδωρ, ὡς Πινδαρος λεγει.
9. ἐσται ἡ ἐσχατη πλανη χειρων της πρωτης.
10. ἐλευθερως δουλευε · δουλος οὐκ ἐσει.

οὐδεις—no one, no
φροντις—thought
ἀμεινων—better⎫
ἀριστος—best ⎭(not N.T.)
ἁπας—all
ἰσχυω—be strong
πως—somehow
χρησμος—oracle

πλανη—error
περισσον—abundantly
ἀναγκη—necessity
βροτος—mortal
ἡμισυ—half
ἐλευθερος—free
ἑκαστος—each

EXERCISE XXIIb

Truly, love is the greatest gift of God to men. Wisdom is good but love is better. He who loves is stronger than his enemy, because he is most able to forgive sins. To love is more than to be a friend. The friend seeks the good of his friend, but he who loves lays down his life for his beloved. The love of Christ is greater than the love of a brother, and the love of God is greater than the love of a father. Those who find it find joy, and find it more abundantly.

(*Note:* * Before a rough breathing τ changes to θ in poetry.)

LESSON XXII

PREPOSITIONS

We have already had several Prepositions which govern various cases. It is time to look at them in logical order and to find some arrangement.

Prepositions were originally adverbs, used to make the meaning of the cases more precise. Most of them answer the questions " when " or " where " and underline the meaning already present in the case.

1. Place—Accusative means motion towards
   Genitive means motion from
   Dative means rest at.

   Thus—εἰς [into] can only be used with Accusative
   ἐκ [out of] „ „ „ „ „ Genitive
   ἐν [in] „ „ „ „ „ Dative.

   Some Prepositions can be used with more than one case.

   Thus—παρα [alongside]—with Accusative—to the side of
   with Genitive—from the side of
   with Dative—at the side of.

2. Time—Accusative means duration over a period
   Genitive means within the course of a period
   Dative means at a point of time.

   Thus—τρεις ἡμερας—for three days
   ἐκεινης της ἡμερας—during that day
   ἐκεινη τη ἡμερα—on that day.

The following are the most important meanings of Prepositions:

1. With one case—α—Accusative
        ἀνα—up
        εἰς—into
    β—Genitive
        ἀντι—over against, instead of
        ἀπο—away from [exterior]
        ἐκ, ἐξ—out of [interior]
        πρo—in front of, before
    γ—Dative
        ἐν—in [time or place]
        συν—together with.

2. With two cases—

	Accusative	*Genitive*
δια [through]	on account of	through, by means of
κατα [down]	according to	against
μετα [amongst]	after	among, with
περι [around]	around [literally]	concerning
ὑπερ [over]	above, beyond	on behalf of
ὑπο [under]	under	by [of agent]

3. With three cases—

	Accusative	*Genitive*	*Dative*
ἐπι [on]	on to, up to	on, in the time of	on, in addition to, at
παρα [beside]	to the side, contrary to	from the side	at the side, near
προς [to]	towards, to	from [rare]	at, close to

(*Note* the following " improper prepositions ":

With Genitive—ἄνευ—without; ἕνεκα—for the sake of; μεχρι—until; χαριν—for the sake of; πλην—except; χωρις—without; ἐμπροσθεν—in front of; ἐντος—within; ἐγγυς—near; ἐνωπιον—in front of.)

AN ADVENTURE WITH A LION

1 προς } τον λεοντα
   παρα

2 προς } τω λεοντι
   παρα

3 ἐπι τον λεοντα

4 περι τον λεοντα

μετα του
λεοντος
συν τω λεοντι

ἀνα τον λεοντα

ὑπερ τον λεοντα

8

ἐπι { τοῦ λέοντος
       τῷ λέοντι

9

κατὰ τὸν λέοντος ᾽

10

ὑπὸ τὸν λέοντα

110

11 εἰς τὸν λέοντα

12 ἐν τῷ λέοντι

13 ἐκ τὸν λέοντος

14 { ἀπὸ τὸν λέοντος
  παρα

Illustrations reproduced from " Teach Yourself Greek "

111

LESSON XXIII

NUMERALS

The following Numerals occur in the New Testament.

Cardinals (one, two, etc.)	Ordinals (first, second, etc.)	Adverbs (once, twice, etc.)	Distributives (single, double, etc.)
1 εἷς	πρωτος, -η, -ον	ἁπαξ	ἁπλους
2 δυο	δευτερος, -α, -ον	δις	διπλους
3 τρεις	τριτος, -η, -ον	τρις	
4 τεσσαρες	τεταρτος, -η, -ον		τετραπλους
5 πεντε	πεμπτος, -η, -ον	πεντακις	
6 ἑξ	ἑκτος, -η, -ον		
7 ἑπτα	ἑβδομος, -η, -ον	ἑπτακις	ἑπταπλασιων
8 ὀκτω	ὀγδοος, -η, -ον		
9 ἐννεα	ἐνατος, -η, -ον		
10 δεκα	δεκατος, -η, -ον		
11 ἑνδεκα	ἑνδεκατος, -η, -ον		
12 δωδεκα [δεκαδυο]	δωδεκατος, -η, -ον		
13			
14 δεκατεσσαρες	τεσσαρεσκαιδεκατος		
15 δεκαπεντε	πεντεκαιδεκατος		
16 δεκαεξ			
17			
18 δεκαοκτω			
19			
20 εἰκοσι		200 διακοσιοι, -αι, -α	
30 τριακοντα		300 τριακοσιοι, -αι, -α	
40 τεσσερακοντα*		400 τετρακοσιοι, -αι, -α	

(*Note:* * in the N.T. τεσσερακοντα always has second vowel ε, though in Classical Greek it is α, as in τεσσαρες.)

50	πεντηκοντα [πεντηκοστος]	500	πεντακοσιοι, -αι, -α
60	ἑξηκοντα	600	ἑξακοσιοι, -αι, -α
70	ἑβδομηκοντα [-κις]		
80	ὀγδοηκοντα		
90	ἐνενηκοντα		
100	ἑκατον [ἑκατονταπλασιων]	1,000	χιλιοι, -αι, -α [χιλιας]
2,000	δισχιλιοι, -αι, -α	10,000	μυριοι, -αι, -α
3,000	τρισχιλιοι, -αι, -α	20,000	δισμυριοι, -αι, -α
4,000	τετρακισχιλιοι, -αι, -α		
5,000	πεντακισχιλιοι, -αι, -α		
7,000	ἑπτακισχιλιοι, -αι, -α		

Note also:

πολλακις—many times
ποσακις—how many times?
πολλαπλασιων—many fold

Cardinals from 1 to 4 are declinable as follows:

	M.	F.	N.	M.F.N.
Nom.	εἱς	μια	ἑν	δυο
Acc.	ἑνα	μιαν	ἑν	δυο
Gen.	ἑνος	μιας	ἑνος	δυο
Dat.	ἑνι	μια	ἑνι	δυσι

	M.F.	N.	M.F.	N.
Nom.	τρεις	τρια	τεσσαρες	τεσσαρα
Acc.	τρεις	τρια	τεσσαρας	τεσσαρα
Gen.	τριων		τεσσαρων	
Dat.	τρισι		τεσσαρσι	

Cardinals from 5 to 199 are not declinable.
Cardinals over 200 and Ordinals are declined like ἀγαθος
οὐδεις and μηδεις (no one) are declined like εἱς—
οὐδεις, οὐδεμια, οὐδεν ; μηδεις, μηδεμια, μηδεν κ.τ.λ.

Compound numbers are expressed as in English, e.g. 253 is διακοσιοι πεντηκοντα τρεις (declinable members must be declined).

Letters were used instead of numbers, and distinguished by accents, α′—1; β′—2; γ′—3 κ.τ.λ. α,—1,000; β, —2,000 κ.τ.λ. But you need not bother about these.

For reference, the full list is as follows:

1—α	10—ι	100—ϱ
2—β	20—κ	200—σ
3—γ	30—λ	300—τ
4—δ	40—μ	400—υ
5—ε	50—ν	500—φ
6—ς	60—ξ	600—χ
7—ζ	70—ο	700—ψ
8—η	80—π	800—ω
9—θ	90— ϙ (koppa)	900—ϡ (sampi)

This can easily be worked out if you remember that with the exception of 6, 90 and 900 you just go through the alphabet, but if you try to do arithmetic with them you will realize why the Greeks only studied geometry amongst the mathematical sciences.

PRONOUNS

Some Pronouns we have already had, and there are a few more.

1. *Personal Pronouns:* First and Second Person— Lesson IX, page 33; Third Person—Lesson VIII, page 31.

   Note: αὐτος is also used idiomatically in two ways, which must be carefully distinguished:

   (*a*) the appropriate form of αὐτο; placed *between the* article and its noun means " same ", e.g.
   the same man—ὁ αὐτος ἀνθρωπος
   of the same woman—της αὐτης γυναικος
   the same books—τα αὐτα βιβλιυ

   (*b*) placed *before the articl·* or *after the noun*, it means " self ", e.g.
   the man himself—αὐτος ὁ ἀνθρωπος
   ὁ ἀνθρωπος αὐτος
   of the woman herself—αὐτης της γυναικος
   της γυναικος αὐτης
   the children themselves—αὐτα τα παιδια
   τα παιδια αὐτα

2. *Possessive Pronouns.* The genitive of the Personal pronoun may be used to express possession, but there are also pronominal adjectives, " mine ", " your ", " our ".

   The singular pronouns have feminine in -η, like κακος, and the plural pronouns have feminine in -α, like ἁγιος.

They must always be accompanied by the article except when used predicatively.

My	ὁ ἐμος	ἡ ἐμη	το ἐμον
Our	ὁ ἡμετερος	ἡ ἡμετερα	το ἡμετερον
Your	ὁ σος	ἡ ση	το σον
Your	ὁ ὑμετερος	ἡ ὑμετερα	το ὑμετερον

There is no third person possessive pronoun.

3. *Reflexive Pronouns.* These are used when the subject's action " reflects " back upon himself, and are formed by combining the pronoun with αὐτος. They have no Nominative case, but this is expressed by adding αὐτος separately with the personal pronoun, e.g. I myself said . . .—ἐγω αὐτος ἐλεγον . . .

	Myself	*Yourself*	*Himself*	*Herself*	*Itself*
Acc.	ἐμαυτον	σεαυτον	ἑαυτον	ἑαυτην	ἑαυτο
Gen.	ἐμαυτου	σεαυτου	ἑαυτου	ἑαυτης	ἑαυτου
Dat.	ἐμαυτῳ	σεαυτῳ	ἑαυτῳ	ἑαυτῃ	ἑαυτῳ

In the Plural there is only one form for " ourselves ", " yourselves " and " themselves ", but it has three genders:

	Masculine	*Feminine*	*Neuter*
Acc.	ἑαυτους	ἑαυτας	ἑαυτα
Gen.	ἑαυτων	ἑαυτων	ἑαυτων
Dat.	ἑαυτοις	ἑαυταις	ἑαυτοις

4. *Reciprocal Pronoun.* This is used when the individual units of a collective subject react. In English we use " each other " or " one another ". This can only be plural, and cannot be nominative.

	Masculine	*Feminine*	*Neuter*
Acc.	ἀλληλους	ἀλληλας	ἀλληλα
Gen.	ἀλληλων	ἀλληλων	ἀλληλων
Dat.	ἀλληλοις	ἀλληλαις	ἀλληλοις

5. *Demonstrative Pronouns.*   (*a*) that—ἐκεινος

Singular

Nom.	ἐκεινος	ἐκεινη	ἐκεινο
Acc.	ἐκεινον	ἐκεινην	ἐκεινο
Gen.	ἐκεινου	ἐκεινης	ἐκεινου
Dat.	ἐκεινῳ	ἐκεινη	ἐκεινῳ

Plural

Nom.	ἐκεινοι	ἐκειναι	ἐκεινα
Acc.	ἐκεινους	ἐκεινας	ἐκεινα
Gen.	ἐκεινων	ἐκεινων	ἐκεινων
Dat.	ἐκεινοις	ἐκειναις	ἐκεινοις

(*b*) this— οὑτος

Singular

Nom.	οὑτος	αὑτη	τουτο
Acc.	τουτον	ταυτην	τουτο
Gen.	τουτου	ταυτης	τουτου
Dat.	τουτῳ	ταυτη	τουτῳ

Plural

Nom.	οὑτοι	αὑται	ταυτα
Acc.	τουτους	ταυτας	ταυτα
Gen.	τουτων	τουτων	τουτων
Dat.	τουτοις	ταυταις	τουτοις

Note: 1. Where οὑτος has -o- or -ω- in the ending it has
-o- in the stem; this means that the genitive
plural feminine is not ταυτων but τουτων.

2. The demonstrative makes the noun definite, and it must therefore have the article. The order is *either* demonstrative, article, noun *or* article, noun, demonstrative but *never* article, demonstrative, noun, e.g.

> οὗτος ὁ ἀνήρ or ὁ ἀνὴρ οὗτος
> BUT NOT ὁ οὗτος ἀνήρ or οὗτος ἀνήρ.

6. *Relative Pronouns* (who, which, that, introducing a relative clause).

	Singular			Plural		
Nom.	ὅς	ἥ	ὅ	οἱ	αἱ	ἅ
Acc.	ὅν	ἥν	ὅ	οὕς	ἅς	ἅ
Gen.	οὗ	ἧς	οὗ	ὧν	ὧν	ὧν
Dat.	ᾧ	ᾗ	ᾧ	οἷς	αἷς	οἷς

Note: The Relative gets its *number* and *gender* from the noun to which it refers, and which is called the antecedent.

The Relative gets its *case* from its function in the relative clause.

7. *Interrogative Pronoun* (who? what?).

| | Singular | | Plural | |
	M.F.	N.	M.F.	N.
Nom.	τίς	τί	τίνες	τίνα
Acc.	τίνα	τί	τίνας	τίνα
Gen.	τίνος	τίνος	τίνων	τίνων
Dat.	τίνι	τίνι	τίσι	τίσι

Note: ὅστις (who) is declined in both parts like ὅς and τις but only nom. is common in the New Testament.

8. *Indefinite Pronoun* (someone, anyone).

This is exactly like the Interrogative τις in form, but can be distinguished because it does not appear as the first word in the sentence, whereas the Interrogative is almost always the first word. In printed Greek the Interrogative has an accent (τίς) whereas the Indefinite has not.

The following list of correlatives will be found useful:

Pronouns

Interrogative		Relative	Demonstrative
Direct	*Indirect*		
τις ; who?	ὅστις—	ὅς—who	οὗτος—this
ποσος : how big?	ὁποσος—	ὅσος—as big as	τοσουτος—so big
ποιος ; of what kind?	ὁποιος—	οἷος—such as	τοιουτος—of such kind

Adverbs

Interrogative		Relative	Indefinite	Demonstrative
Direct	*Indirect*			
που ; where?	ὁπου—	οὗ—where	που—somewhere	ἐκει—there
ποθεν ; whence?	ὁποθεν—	ὅθεν—whence	ποθεν—from somewhere	ἐκειθεν—thence
ποτε ; when?	ὁποτε—	ὅτε—when	ποτε—some time	τοτε—then
πως ; how?	ὁπως—	ὡς—as	πως—somehow	οὕτως—thus

Note:

Direct Interrogatives begin with π-.
Indirect   ,,   ,,   ,,   ὁπ-.
Relatives begin with ὁ-.
Indefinites are like Interrogatives, but enclitic, i.e. they cannot be the first word in the phrase.

LESSON XXV

USE OF THE INFINITIVE

So far our work has mostly consisted of learning the
" accidence " of Greek—that is to say, the formation of
words and their modes of inflection. It is now necessary
to study a little of " syntax ", that is to say, the way in
which words are put together in sentences. We have
mentioned some ways in connection with the Infinitive,
Subjunctive and Participle already, but now we shall look
a little more closely at the Infinitive.

In many cases the Greek Infinitive is used exactly as
the English Infinitive, e.g. in completing the sense of a
noun, adjective or verb:

(a) a time to return—καιρος ἀνακαμψαι.
(b) able to do—δυνατος ποιησαι.
(c) he wishes to go away—θελει ἀπελθειν.
(d) he commanded me to drink—ἐκελευσε με πιειν.
(e) we tried to escape—ἐπειρασαμεν ἀποφυγειν.
(f) he was not able to go—οὐκ ἐδυνατο ἐλθειν.
(g) it is necessary to go away—δει ἀπελθειν.

In all these cases there is no difficulty, but there is one
point which must be noted: when the Infinitive has a subject which is not the subject of the main verb, that subject
is put in the *Accusative* case, e.g. it is necessary for me to
go—δει με ἀπελθειν.

Accusative and Infinitive. This construction is so important that it deserves a heading to itself. It is used
very frequently after verbs of saying, thinking, etc., where
we use a clause introduced by " that ". Instead of using

a clause, the subject of what is said is put in the Accusative, and the verb in the Infinitive: e.g.

How do they say that the Christ is the son of David?
πως λεγουσι τον Χριστον εἰναι υἱον Δαβιδ;

After verbs of preventing this construction is used: e.g.

Do not prevent them from coming to me.
μη κωλυετε αὐτους ἐλθειν προς με.

Articular Infinitive. The Infinitive is a verbal NOUN, and as a noun it can take an article, which is always neuter. It can also be used in different cases, and the article is declined, though the Infinitive remains unchanged. As subject of the sentence it is in the Nominative case, as object in the Accusative, and it may also be used after prepositions, when it takes the appropriate case:

Nom. (*a*) Subject. To work (working) is good for students.
το ἐργαζεσθαι ἀγαθον ἐστι τυις μαθηταις.

Acc. (*b*) Object. I do not refuse to die.
οὐ παραιτουμαι το ἀποθανειν.

Acc. (*c*) After εἰς or προς expressing *purpose.* I went to see him.
ἠλθον προς [εἰς] το θεωρειν αὐτον.

Acc. (*d*) After δια expressing *cause.* Because it had no root it withered.
δια το μη ἐχειν ῥιζαν ἐξηρανθη.

Dat. (*e*) After ἐν expressing *means.* Christ saved us by dying.
ὁ Χριστος ἐσωσεν ἡμας ἐν τῳ ἀποθανειν.

Dat. (*f*) After ἐν expressing *time when.* When he slept, the enemy came.
ἐν τῳ καθευδειν αὐτον ὁ ἐχθρος ἠλθεν.

Gen. (g) After προ expressing *time before*. Before sleeping, you ought to pray.

προ του καθευδειν δει σε προσευχεσθαι.

Acc. (h) After μετα expressing *time after*. After Christ was raised, he appeared to them.

μετα το ἐγερθηναι τον Χριστον ἐφανη αὐτοις.

Consecutive Infinitive. This is used to express the consequence of an action, and is introduced by ὥστε (so that).

I am not so foolish as to believe your excuses.

οὐχ οὕτως μωρος εἰμι ὥστε πιστευειν ταις προφασεσιν ὑμων.

The winds blew, so that the house fell.

οἱ ἀνεμοι ἐπνευσαν ὥστε τον οἰκον πεσειν.

There are a few cases when ὥστε is followed by an Indicative to express an *unexpected* result, e.g. John iii. 16; Galatians ii. 13.

πριν or πριν ἠ [before] is followed by Accusative and Infinitive when the main verb is Affirmative.

πριν ἀλεκτορα φωνησαι τρις ἀπαρνηση με.
Before the cock crows you shall deny me thrice.

EXERCISE XXIIIa

1. τις δ᾽ οἰδεν εἰ το ζην μεν ἐστι κατθανειν,
   το κατθανειν δε ζην κατω νομιζεται ;
2. το ἀγαπαν τον θεον ἐξ ὁλης καρδιας και το ἀγαπαν τον πλησιον ὡς ἑαυτον περισσοτερον ἐστι παντων των ὁλοκαυτωματων και θυσιων.
3. προ γαρ του ἐλθειν τινας ἀπο Ἰακωβου συνησθιεν ὁ Πετρος μετα των ἐθνων.
4. μετα δε το σιγησαι αὐτους ἀπεκριθη Ἰακωβος.
5. οὐκ ἐχετε δια το μη αἰτεισθαι ὑμας.

6. ὁ Ἰησους ἠλθεν εἰς τον κοσμον προς το τους ἁμαρτωλους σωθηναι.

7. κυριε, καταβηθι πριν ἀποθανειν το παιδιον μου.

EXERCISE XXIIIb

Before going to the city it is necessary *to enquire* about the way. *After you have heard* this, you will be able *to make your way* there, but *whilst you are going*, do not speak to anyone. If anyone tells you *to go* into his house, do not listen to him. He will steal your money so that *you will not be able to buy* bread. *Before he seizes* you, run away. The wise man does not believe the fools who say that *there is* much money in the city, *because he knows* that *they are* fools. *To get* money a man *must work, for God said* to Adam that *by working* he must *eat*.

(Translate phrases in italics by using Infinitive constructions.)

LESSON XXVI

USE OF PARTICIPLES

We have already learned something about Participles in Lesson XII (p. 56). It was there noted that the Participle is both a verb and an adjective, and has some of the characteristics of both. Like an adjective it can stand for a noun when the article is added to it.

Participle with Article. Sometimes is the equivalent of a noun and may be translated as such: e.g. ὁ σπειρων— the sower; Ἰωαννης ὁ βαπτιζων—John the baptizer.

Sometimes it is the equivalent of an adjectival clause, and may be translated into English by a relative: e.g.

ὁ μενων ἐν ἀγαπῃ μενει ἐν τῳ Θεῳ.
He who remains in love, remains in God.
τουτο ἐστι το ῥηθεν ὑπο των προφητων.
This is that which was said by the prophets.
οἱ ἀνθρωποι οὐ φιλουσι τους μισουντας αὐτους.
Men do not love those who hate them.
δει με ἐργαζεσθαι τα ἐργα του πεμψαντος με.
I must work the works of him who sent me.

Participle in place of a clause

(a) Relative clause:
πιστευετε εἰς τον δυναμενον σωσαι ὑμας.
Believe in him who is able to save you.

(b) Temporal clause:
πορευομενος παρα την ὁδον εἰδον τον κυνα.
Whilst going along the road I saw the dog.
ἐξελθων ἐκ του οἰκου εἰδον τον κυνα.
After going out of the house I saw the dog.

125

(c) Causal clause:

πάντες ἐφοβοῦντο ἰδόντες το ὅραμα.

They were all afraid because they saw the vision.

(d) Modal clause:

τουτο ποιων τον νομον πληρωσεις.

By doing this you will fulfil the law.

(e) Conditional clause:

πως ἐκφευξομεθα τηλικαυτης ἀμελησαντες σωτηριας ;

How shall we escape if we neglect so great a salvation?

(f) Concessive clause:

καιπερ υἱος ὠν ἐμαθεν την ὑπακοην.

Though he was a Son, he learned obedience.

Genitive Absolute. If the participle is used in any of the above ways, but has a subject which is not connected with any noun or pronoun in the main sentence, the subject and the participle are put into the Genitive case, and the construction is called the Genitive Absolute (from a Latin word which means "not bound", i.e. to the rest of the sentence):

αὐτου εἰποντος τουτο, ἡ γυνη ἀπηλθεν.

When he had said this the woman went away.

ἐκβληθεντος του δαιμονιου ἐλαλησεν ὁ κωφος.

When the devil was cast out, the dumb man spoke.

Note: Greek always preferred to build up sentences by putting one or more participles subordinate to a main verb, rather than a number of main verbs connected by " and " or " but ". This is most noticeable in the New Testament in the writings of Luke. Here is the beginning of Paul's speech at Athens:

᾿Ανδρες ᾿Αθηναιοι, κατα παντα ὡς δεισιδαιμονεστερους ὑμας θεωρω. διερχομενος γαρ και ἀναθεωρων τα σεβασματα ὑμων, εὑρον και βωμον ἐν ᾧ ἐπεγεγραπτο ᾿Αγνωστῳ

Θεῳ. ὁ οὖν ἀγνοουντες εὐσεβειτε τουτο ἐγω καταγγελλω ὑμιν. ὁ Θεος ὁ ποιησας τον κοσμον και παντα τα ἐν αὐτῳ, οὗτος οὐρανου και γης κυριος ὑπαρχων οὐκ ἐν χειροποιητοις ναοις κατοικει · οὐδε ὑπο χειρων ἀνθρωπινων θεραπευεται προσδεομενος τινος, αὐτος διδους πασι ζωην και πνοην και τα παντα.

EXERCISE XXIVa

The following passages are altered from the New Testament, but to find the meaning of words you have not yet had, look at Mark i. ¹⁶ ᶠ and Acts ix.

και παραγων παρα την θαλασσαν της Γαλιλαιας εἰδεν Σιμωνα και Ἀνδρεαν τον ἀδελφον Σιμωνος ἀμφιβαλλοντας ἐν τῃ θαλασσῃ. και εἰπὲν αὐτοις, ἐλθετε ὀπισω μου. και ἀφεντες τα δικτυα ἐπορευοντο ὀπισω του Ἰησου. και παραγοντων αὐτων, Ἰωανης και Ἰακωβος, οἱ του Ζεβεδαιου υἱοι ἠσαν ἐν τῳ πλοιῳ. ὁ δε Ἰησους ἐκαλεσεν αὐτους καταρτιζοντας τα δικτυα. ὁ πατηρ αὐτων Ζεβεδαιος ἰδων τον Ἰησουν ἀφηκεν αὐτους, και εἰπεν, οὐκ ἐγω κωλυσω ὑμας θελοντας συν ἐκεινῳ πορευεσθαι. και εἰσελθων ὁ Ἰησους εἰς την συναγωγην ἠρξατο διδασκειν και ἠν διδασκων αὐτους ὡς ἐξουσιαν ἐχων. και ἐλθοντος ἀνθρωπου τινος ἐν πνευματι ἀκαθαρτῳ οἱ Φαρισαιοι εἰπον, τι ποιησει ; ὁ δε Ἰησους γνους τους διαλογισμους αὐτων ἀπεκριθη λεγων, δια τι συζητειτε προς ἑαυτους λεγοντες τι ποιησει ; ἐν τῳ κοσμῳ μενοντα δει με ἐργαζεσθαι τα ἐργα του πατρος μου. και εἰπεν τῳ ἀνθρωπῳ, ἀναστας ἐλθε προς με. και του Ἰησου λεγοντος, ἐξελθε ἐξ αὐτου, το δαιμονιον σπαραξαν αὐτον ἐξηλθεν.

EXERCISE XXIVb

Translate the words in italics by participles:

Saul, *going* to the high priest asked from him letters

to Damascus. For he wished *to go* there and *find* those who *were* of the Way, and bring them *bound* to Jerusalem. And as he was *drawing near* to Damascus suddenly a light from heaven shone around him. And he heard a voice *saying* to him, Saul, Saul, why are you persecuting me? The men who *were* with him, *hearing* the voice, were afraid, and because they *did not see* anyone they said an angel spoke to him. Saul fell to the ground when he *heard* the voice, and although his eyes *were open* he saw no one. Then a disciple named Ananias, *hearing* a message from the Lord, *rose up* and came to the house where Saul was lodging. When Saul was *praying*, Ananias *came* to the house and went in. Then he *laid* his hands on Saul and said, Jesus, *who appeared* to you on the road, sent me to open your eyes. And when he *laid* his hands on Saul his eyes were opened, and he saw again.

LESSON XXVII

CONDITIONAL SENTENCES

The construction of sentences which express a condition in Greek is quite straightforward, providing that certain points are kept in mind. We have already noted that a condition may be expressed by a Participle (p. 126), but the more common way is by using a clause introduced by εἰ (if), followed by the main clause which expresses the result of the condition. The " if " clause is called the PROTASIS (that which is set out beforehand), and the result-clause is called the APODOSIS (that which is given back, the response).

There are six possible types of conditional sentence, which can be classified in two ways, either with reference to the time to which they refer, or with reference to the probability or otherwise of the fulfilment of the condition.

In reference to time they are PAST, PRESENT and FUTURE.

In reference to fulfilment they are FULFILLED and UN-FULFILLED.

It is important to bear in mind one obvious point: If the condition is either past or present, the result of it is a *fact*, whether it is fulfilled or unfulfilled, whether known or unknown. If fulfilled, it is a positive fact; if unfulfilled, it is a negative fact, but in any case it is a FACT. Therefore, in accordance with the principle noted on page 74, the mood used in Greek must be Indicative. On the other hand, if the condition is future, it is a possibility and not yet a fact, therefore the mood of the verb must be the Subjunctive. If this is borne in mind there will be little difficulty in constructing conditional sentences.

If the Past or Present condition is not fulfilled, the non-fulfilment is a fact, but the sentence also suggests a possibility which might have occurred, but did not. In order to express this, the verb in the Apodosis is qualified with the particle ἄν which cannot be translated, but which indicates a fact which is unfulfilled.

Bearing these points in mind, we can construct any type of Conditional Sentence from the following chart:

TIME	SIMPLE	UNFULFILLED
Past	(If A was, B was) E.g. If I said this, it happened P. εἰ with past indicative A. —past indicative εἰ τουτο εἰπον, ἐγενετο	(If A had been, B would have been) E.g. If I had said this, it would have happened εἰ with aorist indicative—aorist indicative with ἀν εἰ τουτο εἰπον, ἐγενετο ἀν
Present	(If A is, B is) E.g. If I say this, it happens P. εἰ with present indicative— A. present indicative εἰ τουτο λεγω, γινεται	(If A were, B would be) E.g. If I were saying this, it would be happening εἰ with imperfect indicative— imperfect indicative with ἀν εἰ τουτο ἐλεγον, ἐγινετο ἀν
Future	(If A be, B will be) E.g. If I say this, it will happen P. ἐαν with subjunctive— A. future indicative ἐαν εἰπω τουτο, γενησεται	(If A were to be, B would be) E.g. If I were to say this, it would happen εἰ with optative— optative with ἀν εἰ τουτο εἰποιμι, γενοιτο ἀν (THIS TYPE IS NOT IN THE N.T.)

EXERCISE XXVa

1. εἰ κακως ἐλαλησα, εὐθυς μετενοησα.
2. εἰ υἱος εἰ του θεου, καταβηθι ἀπο του σταυρου.
3. εἰ νεκροι οὐκ ἐγειρονται, οὐδε Χριστος ἐγηγερται.
4. εἰ θελεις εἰσελθειν εἰς την ζωην, τηρει τας ἐντολας
5. ἐαν το ἁλας μωρανθῃ, ἐν τινι ἁλισθησεται;
6. ἐαν ἀφητε τοις ἀνθρωποις τα παραπτωματα, ἀφησει και ὑμιν ὁ πατηρ ὑμων ὁ οὐρανιος.
7. ἐαν ᾖ ἐξ ἀνθρωπων ἡ βουλη αὐτη, καταλυθησεται.
8. εἰ ᾔδει ὁ οἰκοδεσποτης ποιᾳ φυλακῃ ὁ κλεπτης ἐρχεται, ἐγρηγορησεν ἀν.
9. Κυριε, εἰ ἦς ὡδε, οὐκ ἀν ἀπεθανεν ὁ ἀδελφος μου.
10. εἰ ἐμε ᾔδειτε, και τον πατερα μου ἀν ᾔδειτε.
11. εἰ τυφλοι ἦτε, οὐκ ἀν εἰχετε ἁμαρτιαν.
12. εἰ ὁ θεος πατηρ ὑμων ἦν, ἠγαπατε ἀν ἐμε.

μετανοεω—repent
ἁλιζω—make salt
βουλη—counsel, plan
φυλακη—watch (of time)
μωραινω—spoil
παραπτωμα—fault, transgression
καταλυω—destroy
γρηγορεω—keep awake

EXERCISE XXVb

1. If the kingdom of heaven were within you, you would know the peace of God in your hearts.
2. If we had done these things we should not have been true servants of God.
3. If the householder knows at what hour the thief comes, he will watch.
4. If you love me, you will keep my commandments.
5. If Jesus had not gone to Jerusalem, he would not have been crucified.
6. Unless your righteousness is more than that of the Pharisees, you can never be saved.

7. If you knew the gift of God and who it is who asks for water, you would ask him and he would give you living water.
8. If I did anything wrong, tell me and I will repent.
9. If I please men, I am not the servant of Christ.
10. If you were truly righteous, you would have known this to be sin.

LESSON XXVIII

OPTATIVE

The Optative mood is rare in the New Testament, but for the sake of completeness it must be learned. Its endings always have a diphthong. It is only found in the New Testament in the Present and Aorist Tenses, and the endings are as follows:

Active:

Present and Second Aorist: -οιμι, -οις, -οι, -οιμεν, -οιτε, -οιεν.

First Aorist: -αιμι, -αις, -αι, -αιμεν, -αιτε, -αιεν.

Middle:

Present and Second Aorist: -οιμην, -οιο, -οιτο, -οιμεθα, -οισθε, -οιντο.

First Aorist: -αιμην, -αιο, -αιτο, -αιμεθα, -αισθε, -αιντο.

Passive:

Present: -οιμην, -οιο, -οιτο, -οιμεθα, -οισθε, -οιντο.

Aorist: -ειην, -ειης, -ειη, -ειμεν, -ειτε, -ειεν.

The Optative of Contracted Verbs in -αω, -εω, and -οω is not found in the New Testament.

The only forms of the Optative of verbs in -μι found in the New Testament are the third person singular aorist optative active of διδωμι which is δῳη, and the optative of εἰμι which is

εἴην	εἴημεν	or εἶμεν
εἴης	εἴητε	or εἶτε
εἴη	εἶεν	

The negative of the Optative is μη.

USES OF OPTATIVE:

1. To express a wish—μη γενοιτο. May it not happen, God forbid!

   ἰδου, ἡ δουλη Κυριου · γενοιτο μοι κατα το ῥημα σου.

   Behold the handmaid of the Lord; may it be to me according to thy word.

   το ἀργυριον συν σοι εἰη εἰς ἀπωλειαν.

   May you and your money perish.

2. In dependent questions—(with ἀν)

   This usage is only found in Luke and Acts, and is almost exclusively used in the phrase τι ἀν εἰη, τις ἀν εἰη.

   ἀκουσας δε ὀχλου διαπορευομενου, ἐπυνθανετο τι ἀν εἰη τουτο.

   Hearing the crowd going by, he asked what this might be.

3. In Conditional Sentences—

   There is an incomplete example in 1 Peter iii. 14 of a remote future condition, in which only the Protasis occurs:

   ἀλλ᾽ εἰ και πασχοιτε δια δικαιοσυνην, μακαριοι.

   But even if you should suffer for righteousness' sake, blessed are you.

   (Cf. also 1 Peter iii. 17 and Acts xx. 16.)

4. Potential Optative—

   There are three examples of an optative used to express what would or might possibly be.

   πως γαρ ἀν δυναιμην, ἐαν μη τις ὁδηγησει με ;

   How could I, unless someone guides me?

5. After πριν when the main clause is negative—

   There is one example of this in Acts xxv. 16.

οὐ AND μή

The following points may be noted about the use of
οὐ and μή:

1. Normally οὐ negatives facts and μή negatives possibilities.
2. οὐ almost always negatives the Indicative, the only exception in the New Testament being in the Protasis of unfulfilled conditions, where the negative is usually μή.
3. μή always negatives Imperative, Subjunctive and Optative.
4. μή almost always negatives Participles and Infinitives, but there are a few exceptions. (There are about seventeen uses of οὐ with a Participle.)
5. In clauses introduced by μή meaning " lest " the negative is οὐ even though the verb is in the Subjunctive.
6. Compound negatives.

   If a compound negative follows a simple negative they strengthen one another, otherwise they cancel out.

   E.g. οὐχ ὁρᾳ οὐδεις—no one at all sees; οὐδεις οὐχ ὁρᾳ—everyone sees.

Tense with Stem	Indicative		Imperative
	Primary	Historic	
PRESENT ACTIVE λv-	λv-ω λv-$\varepsilon \iota \varsigma$ λv-$\varepsilon \iota$ λv-$o \mu \varepsilon v$ λv-$\varepsilon \tau \varepsilon$ λv-$o v \sigma \iota$	$\dot{\varepsilon}$-λv-$o v$ $\dot{\varepsilon}$-λv-$\varepsilon \varsigma$ $\dot{\varepsilon}$-λv-ε $\dot{\varepsilon}$-λv-$o \mu \varepsilon v$ $\dot{\varepsilon}$-λv-$\varepsilon \tau \varepsilon$ $\dot{\varepsilon}$-λv-$o v$	λv-ε λv-$\varepsilon \tau \omega$ λv-$\varepsilon \tau \varepsilon$ λv-$\varepsilon \tau \omega \sigma \alpha v$
FUTURE ACTIVE $\lambda v \sigma$-	$\lambda v \sigma$-ω $\lambda v \sigma$-$\varepsilon \iota \varsigma$ $\lambda v \sigma$-$\varepsilon \iota$ $\lambda v \sigma$-$o \mu \varepsilon v$ $\lambda v \sigma$-$\varepsilon \tau \varepsilon$ $\lambda v \sigma$-$o v \sigma \iota$		
FIRST AORIST ACTIVE [WEAK] $\lambda v \sigma \alpha$-		$\dot{\varepsilon}$-$\lambda v \sigma$-α $\dot{\varepsilon}$-$\lambda v \sigma$-$\alpha \varsigma$ $\dot{\varepsilon}$-$\lambda v \sigma$-ε $\dot{\varepsilon}$-$\lambda v \sigma$-$\alpha \mu \varepsilon v$ $\dot{\varepsilon}$-$\lambda v \sigma$-$\alpha \tau \varepsilon$ $\dot{\varepsilon}$-$\lambda v \sigma$-αv	$\lambda v \sigma$-$o v$ $\lambda v \sigma$-$\alpha \tau \omega$ $\lambda v \sigma$-$\alpha \tau \varepsilon$ $\lambda v \sigma$-$\alpha \tau \omega \sigma \alpha v$
SECOND AORIST ACTIVE [STRONG] [$\lambda \alpha \beta$-]		$\dot{\varepsilon}$-$\lambda \alpha \beta$-$o v$ $\dot{\varepsilon}$-$\lambda \alpha \beta$-$\varepsilon \varsigma$ $\dot{\varepsilon}$-$\lambda \alpha \beta$-ε $\dot{\varepsilon}$-$\lambda \alpha \beta$-$o \mu \varepsilon v$ $\dot{\varepsilon}$-$\lambda \alpha \beta$-$\varepsilon \tau \varepsilon$ $\dot{\varepsilon}$-$\lambda \alpha \beta$-$o v$	$\lambda \alpha \beta$-ε $\lambda \alpha \beta$-$\varepsilon \tau \omega$ $\lambda \alpha \beta$-$\varepsilon \tau \varepsilon$ $\lambda \alpha \beta$-$\varepsilon \tau \omega \sigma \alpha v$
PERFECT ACTIVE $\lambda \varepsilon$-$\lambda v \varkappa$-	$\lambda \varepsilon$-$\lambda v \varkappa$-α $\lambda \varepsilon$-$\lambda v \varkappa$-$\alpha \varsigma$ $\lambda \varepsilon$-$\lambda v \varkappa$-ε $\lambda \varepsilon$-$\lambda v \varkappa$-$\alpha \mu \varepsilon v$ $\lambda \varepsilon$-$\lambda v \varkappa$-$\alpha \tau \varepsilon$ $\lambda \varepsilon$-$\lambda v \varkappa$-$\alpha \sigma \iota$	$\dot{\varepsilon}$-$\lambda \varepsilon$-$\lambda v \varkappa$-$\varepsilon \iota v$ $\dot{\varepsilon}$-$\lambda \varepsilon$-$\lambda v \varkappa$-$\varepsilon \iota \varsigma$ $\dot{\varepsilon}$-$\lambda \varepsilon$-$\lambda v \varkappa$-$\varepsilon \iota$ $\dot{\varepsilon}$-$\lambda \varepsilon$-$\lambda v \varkappa$-$\varepsilon \iota \mu \varepsilon v$ $\dot{\varepsilon}$-$\lambda \varepsilon$-$\lambda v \varkappa$-$\varepsilon \iota \tau \varepsilon$ $\dot{\varepsilon}$-$\lambda \varepsilon$-$\lambda v \varkappa$-$\varepsilon \iota \sigma \alpha v$	$\lambda \varepsilon$-$\lambda v \varkappa$-ε $\lambda \varepsilon$-$\lambda v \varkappa$-$\varepsilon \tau \omega$ $\lambda \varepsilon$-$\lambda v \varkappa$-$\varepsilon \tau \varepsilon$ $\lambda \varepsilon$-$\lambda v \varkappa$-$\varepsilon \tau \omega \sigma \alpha v$
PRESENT MIDDLE AND PASSIVE λv-	λv-$o \mu \alpha \iota$ λv-η λv-$\varepsilon \tau \alpha \iota$ λv-$o \mu \varepsilon \theta \alpha$ λv-$\varepsilon \sigma \theta \varepsilon$ λv-$o v \tau \alpha \iota$	$\dot{\varepsilon}$-λv-$o \mu \eta v$ $\dot{\varepsilon}$-λv-$o v$ $\dot{\varepsilon}$-λv-$\varepsilon \tau o$ $\dot{\varepsilon}$-λv-$o \mu \varepsilon \theta \alpha$ $\dot{\varepsilon}$-λv-$\varepsilon \sigma \theta \varepsilon$ $\dot{\varepsilon}$-λv-$o v \tau o$	λv-$o v$ λv-$\varepsilon \sigma \theta \omega$ λv-$\varepsilon \sigma \theta \varepsilon$ λv-$\varepsilon \sigma \theta \omega \sigma \alpha v$

OF λύω

SUBJUNCTIVE PRIMARY	OPTATIVE HISTORIC	INFINITIVE VERBAL NOUN	PARTICIPLE VERBAL ADJECTIVE	
λυ-ω λυ-ῃς λυ-ῃ λυ-ωμεν λυ-ητε λυ-ωσι	λυ-οιμι λυ-οις λυ-οι λυ-οιμεν λυ-οιτε λυ-οιεν	λυ-ειν	λυ-ων λυ-ουσα λυ-ον	
	λυσ-οιμι λυσ-οις λυσ-οι λυσ-οιμεν λυσ-οιτε λυσ-οιεν	λυσ-ειν	λυσ-ων λυσ-ουσα λυσ-ον	
λυσ-ω λυσ-ῃς λυσ-ῃ λυσ-ωμεν λυσ-ητε λυσ-ωσι	λυσ-αιμι λυσ-αις λυσ-αι λυσ-αιμεν λυσ-αιτε λυσ-αιεν	λυσ-αι	λυσ-ας λυσ-ασα λυσ-αν	
λαβ-ω λαβ-ῃς λαβ-ῃ λαβ-ωμεν λαβ-ητε λαβ-ωσι	λαβ-οιμι λαβ-οις λαβ-οι λαβ-οιμεν λαβ-οιτε λαβ-οιεν	λαβ-ειν	λαβ-ων λαβ-ουσα λαβ-ον	[FROM THE VERB λαμβανω]
λε-λυκ-ω λε-λυκ-ῃς λε-λυκ-ῃ λε-λυκ-ωμεν λε-λυκ-ητε λε-λυκ-ωσι	λε-λυκ-οιμι λε-λυκ-οις λε-λυκ-οι λε-λυκ-οιμεν λε-λυκ-οιτε λε-λυκ-οιεν	λε-λυκ-εναι	λε-λυκ-ως λε-λυκ-υια λε-λυκ-ος	
λυ-ωμαι λυ-ῃ λυ-ηται λυ-ωμεθα λυ-ησθε λυ-ωνται	λυ-οιμην λυ-οιο λυ-οιτο λυ-οιμεθα λυ-οισθε λυ-οιντο	λυ-εσθαι	λυ-ομενος λυ-ομενη λυ-ομενον	

Tense with Stem	Indicative		Imperative
	Primary	Historic	
FUTURE MIDDLE $\lambda\upsilon\sigma$-	$\lambda\upsilon\sigma$-ομαι $\lambda\upsilon\sigma$-η $\lambda\upsilon\sigma$-εται $\lambda\upsilon\sigma$-ομεθα $\lambda\upsilon\sigma$-εσθε $\lambda\upsilon\sigma$-ονται		
FIRST AORIST MIDDLE [WEAK] $\lambda\upsilon\sigma a$-		ἐ-$\lambda\upsilon\sigma$-αμην ἐ-$\lambda\upsilon\sigma$-ω ἐ-$\lambda\upsilon\sigma$-ατο ἐ-$\lambda\upsilon\sigma$-αμεθα ἐ-$\lambda\upsilon\sigma$-ασθε ἐ-$\lambda\upsilon\sigma$-αντο	$\lambda\upsilon\sigma$-αι $\lambda\upsilon\sigma$-ασθω $\lambda\upsilon\sigma$-ασθε $\lambda\upsilon\sigma$-ασθωσαν
SECOND AORIST MIDDLE [STRONG] [λαβ-]		ἐ-λαβ-ομην ἐ-λαβ-ου ἐ-λαβ-ετο ἐ-λαβ-ομεθα ἐ-λαβ-εσθε ἐ-λαβ-οντο	λαβ-ου λαβ-εσθω λαβ-εσθε λαβ-εσθωσαν
PERFECT MIDDLE AND PASSIVE $\lambda\varepsilon$-$\lambda\upsilon$-	$\lambda\varepsilon$-$\lambda\upsilon$-μαι $\lambda\varepsilon$-$\lambda\upsilon$-σαι $\lambda\varepsilon$-$\lambda\upsilon$-ται $\lambda\varepsilon$-$\lambda\upsilon$-μεθα $\lambda\varepsilon$-$\lambda\upsilon$-σθε $\lambda\varepsilon$-$\lambda\upsilon$-νται	ἐ-$\lambda\varepsilon$-$\lambda\upsilon$-μην ἐ-$\lambda\varepsilon$-$\lambda\upsilon$-σο ἐ-$\lambda\varepsilon$-$\lambda\upsilon$-το ἐ-$\lambda\varepsilon$-$\lambda\upsilon$-μεθα ἐ-$\lambda\varepsilon$-$\lambda\upsilon$-σθε ἐ-$\lambda\varepsilon$-$\lambda\upsilon$-ντο	$\lambda\varepsilon$-$\lambda\upsilon$-σο $\lambda\varepsilon$-$\lambda\upsilon$-σθω $\lambda\varepsilon$-$\lambda\upsilon$-σθε $\lambda\varepsilon$-$\lambda\upsilon$-σθωσαν
FIRST AORIST PASSIVE [WEAK] $\lambda\upsilon\theta\eta$-		ἐ-$\lambda\upsilon\theta$-ην ἐ-$\lambda\upsilon\theta$-ης ἐ-$\lambda\upsilon\theta$-η ἐ-$\lambda\upsilon\theta$-ημεν ἐ-$\lambda\upsilon\theta$-ητε ἐ-$\lambda\upsilon\theta$-ησαν	$\lambda\upsilon\theta$-ητι $\lambda\upsilon\theta$-ητω $\lambda\upsilon\theta$-ητε $\lambda\upsilon\theta$-ητωσαν
FUTURE PASSIVE $\lambda\upsilon\theta\eta\sigma$-	$\lambda\upsilon\theta$-ησ-ομαι $\lambda\upsilon\theta$-ησ-η $\lambda\upsilon\theta$-ησ-εται $\lambda\upsilon\theta$-ησ-ομεθα $\lambda\upsilon\theta$-ησ-εσθε $\lambda\upsilon\theta$-ησ-ονται		

Notes: Perfect Subjunctive and Optative, Middle and Passive, are formed by using the Subjunctive and Optative of εἰμι with the Perfect Participle Passive. This is called a " Periphrastic " Tense.

OF λυω (continued)

SUBJUNCTIVE PRIMARY	OPTATIVE HISTORIC	INFINITIVE VERBAL NOUN	PARTICIPLE VERBAL ADJECTIVE	
	λυσ-οιμην λυσ-οιο λυσ-οιτο λυσ-οιμεθα λυσ-οισθε λυσ-οιντο	λυσ-εσθαι	λυσ-ομενος λυσ-ομενη λυσ-ομενον	
λυσ-ωμαι λυσ-η λυσ-ηται λυσ-ωμεθα λυσ-ησθε λυσ-ωνται	λυσ-αιμην λυσ-αιο λυσ-αιτο λυσ-αιμεθα λυσ-αισθε λυσ-αιντο	λυσ-ασθαι	λυσ-αμενος λυσ-αμενη λυσ-αμενον	
λαβ-ωμαι λαβ-η λαβ-ηται λαβ-ωμεθα λαβ-ησθε λαβ-ωνται	λαβ-οιμην λαβ-οιο λαβ-οιτο λαβ-οιμεθα λαβ-οισθε λαβ-οιντο	λαβ-εσθαι	λαβ-ομενος λαβ-ομενη λαβ-ομενον	[FROM THE VERB λαμβανω]
[SEE NOTE BELOW]	[SEE NOTE BELOW]	λε-λυ-σθαι	λε-λυ-μενος λε-λυ-μενη λε-λυ-μενον	
λυθ-ω λυθ-ης λυθ-η λυθ-ωμεν λυθ-ητε λυθ-ωσι	λυθ-ειην λυθ-ειης λυθ-ειη λυθ-ειμεν λυθ-ειτε λυθ-ειεν	λυθ-ηναι	λυθ-εις λυθ-εισα λυθ-εν	
	λυθ-ησ-οιμην λυθ-ησ-οιο λυθ-ησ-οιτο λυθ-ησ-οιμεθα λυθ-ησ-οισθε λυθ-ησ-οιντο	λυθ-ησ-εσθαι	λυθ-ησ-ομενος λυθ-ησ-ομενη λυθ-ησ-ομενον	

The Second Aorist Passive is exactly like the First Aorist Passive without -θ-, but in the second singular imperative the ending is -θι instead of -τι, e.g. σπαρηθι.

All Aorist Passive endings are like Active endings.

LIST OF VERBS

(*Note:* This list is not exhaustive but gives the most common verbs in the New Testament. The arrangement in groups could be much more elaborate but would not greatly help the ordinary student. The only satisfactory way to deal with them is to learn off the Principal Parts as given until they come automatically.)

PRESENT ACTIVE	FUTURE ACTIVE	AORIST ACTIVE	PERFECT ACTIVE	PERFECT PASSIVE	AORIST PASSIVE	MEANING
GROUP I—VERBS GENERALLY LIKE λύω, BUT WITH IRREGULARITIES						
1. ἄγω	ἄξω	ἤγαγον	ἦχα	ἦγμαι	ἤχθην	lead
2. ἀκούω	ἀκούσω / ἀκούσομαι	ἤκουσα	ἀκήκοα		ἠκούσθην	hear
3. ἁμαρτάνω	ἁμαρτήσω	ἥμαρτον / ἡμάρτησα	ἡμάρτηκα			sin
4. ἀνοίγω	ἀνοίξω	ἀνέῳξα / ἠνέῳξα / ἤνοιξα	ἀνέῳγα	ἀνέῳγμαι / ἠνέῳγμαι / ἤνοιγμαι	ἀνεῴχθην / ἠνεῴχθην / ἠνοίχθην	open
5. ἀποθνῄσκω	ἀποθανοῦμαι	ἀπέθανον	τέθνηκα			die
6. ἀποκαλύπτω	ἀποκαλύψω	ἀπεκάλυψα			ἀπεκαλύφθην	reveal
7. ἀρέσκω	ἀρέσω	ἤρεσα				please
8. αὐξάνω	αὐξήσω	ηὔξησα			ηὐξήθην	increase
9. βαπτίζω	βαπτίσω	ἐβάπτισα		βεβάπτισμαι	ἐβαπτίσθην	baptize
10. βαίνω	βήσομαι	ἔβην	βέβηκα			go
11. β...	β...	...α...				see

Present	Future	Aorist	Perfect Act.	Perfect M/P	Aorist Pass.	Meaning
13. γράφω	γράψω	ἔγραψα	γέγραφα	γέγραμμαι	ἐγράφην	write
14. διδάσκω	διδάξω	ἐδίδαξα			ἐδιδάχθην	teach
15. ἐκκόπτω	ἐκκόψω	ἐξέκοψα			ἐξεκόπην	cut out
16. εὑρίσκω	εὑρήσω	εὗρον	εὕρηκα		εὑρέθην	find
17. θέλω	θελήσω	ἠθέλησα				will, wish
18. καταλείπω	καταλείψω	κατέλιπον				leave
19. κηρύσσω	κηρύξω	ἐκήρυξα	κεκήρυχα	κεκήρυγμαι	ἐκηρύχθην	preach, herald
20. κράζω	{ κράξω / κεκράξομαι	ἔκραξα	κέκραγα			cry out
21. κρύπτω	κρύψω	ἔκρυψα	κέκρυφα	κέκρυμμαι	{ ἐκρύφθην / ἐκρύβην	hide
22. λαμβάνω	λήμψομαι	ἔλαβον	εἴληφα	εἴλημμαι	ἐλήμφθην	take
23. μανθάνω	μαθήσομαι	ἔμαθον	μεμάθηκα			learn
24. πείθω	πείσω	ἔπεισα	πέποιθα	πέπεισμαι	ἐπείσθην	persuade
25. πέμπω	πέμψω	ἔπεμψα			ἐπέμφθην	send
26. πίνω	πίομαι	ἔπιον	πέπωκα		ἐπόθην	drink
27. πίπτω	πεσοῦμαι	ἔπεσον	πέπτωκα			fall
28. πιστεύω	πιστεύσω	ἐπίστευσα	πεπίστευκα	πεπίστευμαι	ἐπιστεύθην	believe
29. πράσσω	πράξω	ἔπραξα	πέπραχα	πέπραγμαι	ἐπράχθην	do, practise
30. σῴζω	σώσω	ἔσωσα	σέσωκα	σέσωσμαι	ἐσώθην	save
31. τίκτω	τέξομαι	ἔτεκον			ἐτέχθην	bring forth child
32. τρέφω	θρέψω	ἔθρεψα		τέθραμμαι	ἐτράφην	nurture
33. τυγχάνω	τεύξομαι	ἔτυχον				happen
34. φεύγω	φεύξομαι	ἔφυγον				flee

LIST OF VERBS (continued)

	PRESENT ACTIVE	FUTURE ACTIVE	AORIST ACTIVE	PERFECT ACTIVE	PERFECT PASSIVE	AORIST PASSIVE	MEANING
		GROUP II—LIQUID VERBS (STEMS IN λ, ν, ρ)					
35.	ἀγγελλω	ἀγγελῶ	ἤγγειλα		ἤγγελμαι	ἠγγέλην	announce
36.	βαλλω	βαλῶ	ἔβαλον	βέβληκα	βέβλημαι	ἐβλήθην	throw
37.	στελλω	στελῶ	ἔστειλα	ἔσταλκα	ἔσταλμαι	ἐστάλην	send
38.	ἀποκτεινω	ἀποκτενῶ	ἀπέκτεινα			ἀπεκτάνθην	kill
39.	κερδαινω	{ κερδανῶ / κερδήσω	{ ἐκέρδανα / ἐκέρδησα				gain
40.	κλινω	κλινῶ	ἔκλινα	κέκλικα		ἐκλίθην	lean
41.	κρινω	κρινῶ	ἔκρινα	κέκρικα	κέκριμαι	ἐκρίθην	judge
42.	μενω	μενῶ	ἔμεινα	μεμένηκα			remain
43.	φαινω	φανῶ	ἤρα			ἐφάνην	show forth
44.	αἰρω	ἀρῶ	ἤρα	ἦρκα	ἦρμαι	ἤρθην	take away
45.	ἐγειρω	ἐγερῶ	ἤγειρα		ἐγήγερμαι	ἠγέρθην	rouse, raise
46.	σπειρω	σπερῶ	ἔσπειρα		ἔσπαρμαι	ἐσπάρην	sow
47.	φθειρω	φθερῶ	ἔφθειρα			ἐφθάρην	destroy
48.	χαιρω	χαρήσομαι				ἐχάρην	rejoice

(*Note:* All Future Active except χαρήσομαι are contracted endings.)

	PRESENT ACTIVE	FUTURE ACTIVE	AORIST ACTIVE	PERFECT ACTIVE	PERFECT PASSIVE	AORIST PASSIVE	MEANING
		GROUP III—DEPONENT VERBS					
49.	ἀποκρινομαι		ἀπεκρινάμην			ἀπεκρίθην	answer
50.	ἀρχομαι	ἀρξομαι	ἠρξάμην				begin
51.	βουλομαι	βουλήσομαι				{ ἐβουλήθην / ἠβουλήθην	wish

53.						
54. δυναμαι	δυνησομαι				ηδυνηθην	be able
55. θεαομαι	θεασομαι	εθεασαμην		τεθεαμαι		behold
56. ιαομαι		ιασαμην			ιαθην	heal
57. φοβεομαι	φοβηθησομαι				εφοβηθην	fear

Note: All meanings are Active, whether forms are Middle or Passive, except ιαθην and εδεχθην which are Passive.

GROUP IV—CONTRACTED VERBS

58. τιμαω	τιμησω	ετιμησα	τετιμηκα	τετιμημαι	ετιμηθην	honour

(Most -αω verbs follow this pattern: the chief exceptions are:)

59. εαω	εασω	ειασα				allow
60. ζαω	ζησω / ζησομαι	εζησα				live
61. πειναω	πεινασω	επεινασα				hunger
62. ποιεω	ποιησω	εποιησα	πεποιηκα	πεποιημαι	εποιηθην	make, do

(Most -εω verbs follow this pattern: the chief exceptions are:)

63. δοκεω		εδοξα				seem
64. καλεω	καλεσω	εκαλεσα	κεκληκα	κεκλημαι	εκληθην	call
65. τελεω	τελεσω	ετελεσα	τετελεκα	τετελεσμαι	ετελεσθην	complete
66. πληροω	πληρωσω	επληρωσα	πεπληρωκα	πεπληρωμαι	επληρωθην	fill

(All -οω verbs follow this pattern.)

GROUP V—VERBS IN -μι

67. απολλυμι } απολλυω	απολεσω	απολεσα απωλομην*	απολωλα*			destroy
68. αφιημι	αφησω	αφηκα		αφεωνται (3rd plural)	αφεθην	forgive, let go, allow

* In Passive sense—"perish".

LIST OF VERBS (continued)

Present Active	Future Active	Aorist Active	Perfect Active	Perfect Passive	Aorist Passive	Meaning
69. δείκνυμι / δεικνύω	δείξω	ἔδειξα				show
70. δίδωμι	δώσω	ἔδωκα	δέδωκα	δέδομαι	ἐδόθην	give
71. εἰμί	ἔσομαι	ἦν (Impf.)				be
72. ἵστημι	στήσω	ἔστησα / ἔστην	ἕστηκα	ἕσταμαι	ἐστάθην	cause to stand
73. τίθημι	θήσω	ἔθηκα	τέθηκα	τέθειμαι	ἐτέθην	place
74. φημί		ἔφην (Impf.)				say

GROUP VI.—DEFECTIVE VERBS

Present Active	Future Active	Aorist Active	Perfect Active	Perfect Passive	Aorist Passive	Meaning
75. ἀναιρέω	ἀνελῶ	ἀνεῖλον			ἀνῃρέθην	take up, kill
76. ἔρχομαι	ἐλεύσομαι	ἦλθον / ἦλθα	ἐλήλυθα			come, go
77. ἐσθίω	φάγομαι	ἔφαγον				eat
78. ἔχω	ἕξω	ἔσχον	ἔσχηκα			have
79. λέγω	λέξω / ἐρῶ	ἔλεξα / εἶπον / εἶπα	εἴρηκα	λέλεγμαι / εἴρημαι	ἐλέχθην / ἐρρήθην / ἐρρέθην	say
80. ὁράω	ὄψομαι	εἶδον	ἑώρακα / ἑόρακα		ὤφθην	see
81. πάσχω		ἔπαθον	πέπονθα			suffer
82. τρέχω		ἔδραμον				run
83. φέρω	οἴσω	ἤνεγκον / ἤνεγκα	ἐνήνοχα		ἠνέχθην	carry

KEY TO EXERCISES

Ia

1. The man is good.
2. The good teacher writes the words.
3. The girl sees the face of the bad man (the bad man's face).
4. The brother snatches the slave's garment.
5. God watches over the world.
    (God is reckoned as a proper name and therefore has article.)
6. The word of the scripture (writing) is good.
7. The book is in the bag.
8. The man is sitting on the chair.

Ib

1. ἡ κορη ἐστιν ἀγαθη.
2. ὁ κακος ἀνθρωπος βλεπει την ἀγαθην κορην.
3. το του διδασκαλου βιβλιον ἐστιν ἀγαθον.
4. ἡ κορη λεγει λογον τῳ ἀδελφῳ.
5. ἀνθρωπε, ὁ θεος ἐστιν ἀγαθος.

II

neologism—a word which is newly-coined.

economy—(the first diphthong becomes " oe " in Latin, then in English shortens to " e ").

tyrant—(not originally in a bad sense, but since autocratic rule corrupts it tended to collect a bad sense).

democracy—the rule of the people.

cryptograph—something written in a secret code.

angel—(originally any messenger, but the New Testament usage confined it to heavenly messengers later).

idol—an image of the god or goddess.

hymn—

hierarchy—an arrangement of priestly rulers (though it is now often used for any system of rulers).

monarchy—the rule of one man.

Mesopotamia—the land between the Tigris and Euphrates.

throne—

theology—talking about God.

macrocosm—the universe as a whole (we also use " microcosm ").

homoeopathy—the treatment of disease by like things.

zoology—the science of animals.

orthodoxy—going according to the right opinion.

philosophy—the love of wisdom.

autograph—that which a man writes himself.

palaeography—the study of ancient writing.

Philadelphia—the city of brotherly love.

aristocracy—the rule of the best people.

chlorophyll—the substance which makes leaves green.

microscope—the instrument for looking at the very small.

anemometer—the instrument for measuring the wind.

biology—the science of life.

microphone—a means of making a small sound into a big one.

cycle—(this is an interesting example of transliteration).

megaphone—an instrument for making a big sound.

Sentences from Greek authors in Lesson V

1. A big book is a big evil.
2. The unexamined life is not livable for man.
3. Man is a political animal.
   (Aristotle meant the kind of animal who lives in cities.)
4. The friend is another self.
5. Time educates the wise.
6. In the beginning was the Word and the Word was with God and the Word was God.
7. I am the Alpha and the Omega, the beginning and the ending, the first and the last.

IIIa

1. The tree is good.
2. God loves the good (men).
3. The children were in the river.
4. The fear of the Lord is the beginning of wisdom.
5. The people do not keep the word of God.

   (In English " people " is treated as a plural, but in Greek λαος is a collective noun, grammatically singular.)

IIIb

6. τα δαιμονια ἐστιν ἐν τῳ κοσμῳ.
7. ὁ ἀποστολος βλεπει τα των παιδιων βιβλια.
8. ὁ βιος (ἡ ζωη) των ἀνθρωπων ἐστιν ἀγαθος (ἀγαθη).
9. ὁ θανατος ἐστι κυριος των ἀνθρωπων.

   (θανατος and ἀνθρωπων are both nouns referring to a class, therefore have the article.)
10. το παιδιον ἐστιν ἐν τῳ πλοιῳ.

IVa

1. The tongue is the cause of many evils.

   (This is a line of poetry, therefore πολλων is changed in the order to fit in with the rhythm.)
2. Life is short, art is long.

   (The verb " to be " is often omitted in Greek when it merely serves to join a subject and predicate.)
3. The good friend is a physician of grief.

   (Note inversion of order for poetry.)
4. God is love and he who remains in love remains in God, and God in him.
5. Righteousness and truth and love are in the kingdom of God.

   (Abstract nouns take an article.)

IVb

6. ἡ εἰρηνη του θεου τηρει τας ψυχας ἐν τη γη.

   (θεου and γη both refer to a class, since each of them is unique, therefore they have the article.)

147

7. ὁ θεος βλεπει την λυπην των καρδιων των ἀνθρωπων και σωζει αὐτους.
8. ὁ κοσμος ἐστιν ἐν τη ἁμαρτια και οὐκ ἐχει την ἀγαπην.
9. ὁ ἀποστολος γραφει τας γραφας.
10. ἡ φωνη του κυριου λαλει λογους της ἀληθειας.

Va

1. Beloved, I am not writing to you a new commandment, but an old commandment.
2. The old commandment is the word which you heard.
3. Children, it is the last hour.
4. In this are clear the children of God and the children of the devil.
5. His commandment is eternal life.
6. The man is not from God because he does not keep the Sabbath.
7. I am the way and the truth and the life.
8. Many first shall be last, and the last first.
9. The end of the commandment is love out of a pure heart.
10. God rested on the seventh day from all his works.

Vb

ὁ βιος ληστου . . . ἀγαπην . . . δοξαν . . . ἐν τη καρδια αὐτου . . . την λυπην . . . ἐχει τεχνην . . . ἐν τω ἐργω αὐτου . . . ληστης . . . τελωνην . . . ὁ ἀνθρωπος . . . πηραν . . . ἐν τη πηρα . . . χρυσος . . . ὁ ληστης . . . ὁ ἀλλος ἀνθρωπος . . . ὁ τελωνης . . . την κεφαλην . . . τον ληστην . . . τον χρυσον . . . χαρτην . . . ὁ νομος . . . ἡ τεχνη . . . τον χρυσον, δεσποτα.

VI

When a man says that he is good, I know that he is a liar. Sin remains in men and we do not find a good man in the world. When men judge others, they say that the students do not learn, the friends of the doctors die, the tax-collectors steal. If you listen to the critics, you believe that there is no man just and worthy of glory. God is good, men are wicked and hypocrites. They take the things of others, they eat and drink. But God knows the sins of men and saves them. Men die in their sins, but God raises the dead; if we believe, we have salvation.

(Note in the last sentence—" their sins "; since it is clear from the context whose sins are mentioned the article alone is used and " their " is not expressed in Greek.)

VIIa

On the seventh day we shall lead the children to the trees, and we shall teach them the mysteries of the earth. They will see the fruits and the leaves. In the fields the slaves will guard the flocks and the good slave will save them from the robbers.

VIIb

ἐν τῃ ἐσχατῃ ἡμερᾳ ὁ κριτης του κοσμου καθισει ἐν τοις οὐρανοις και οἱ ἀγγελοι ἀξουσι τους ἀνθρωπους. ἀκουσεις τον λογον των ἁμαρτιων σου και βλεψεις την δικαιοσυνην του θεου. σωσει σε ἀπο της ἀπωλειας και ἐλεησει σε. οὐδεις ἀξιος ἐστι της ἀγαπης αὐτου ἀλλα βλεψομεν την δοξαν αὐτου και πιστευσομεν εἰς αὐτον.

VIIIa

Happy is the man who keeps the commandments of God; he will save his soul in the last day. But he who does not keep (them) will see the wrath of God. For we know that the angels will write the works of men in the book of life. God will judge the world according to their works and will send men to their reward. He will send the good to life and the bad to destruction.

VIIIb

ὁ διδασκαλος διδαξει τους μαθητας την ἀληθειαν (note: διδασκω takes a double accusative, of the person and the thing), ἀλλα οἱ μαθηται οὐκ ἀκουσουσι. ἐπιθυμησουσι την σοφιαν, ἀλλ᾽ οὐ ποιησουσι τα ἐργα της σοφιας. τοτε ὁ διδασκαλος λεξει, " ζητησετε με, ἀλλ᾽ οὐκ ἀξω ὑμας προς την σοφιαν ". οἱ λογοι του διδασκαλου μενουσιν ἐν ταις καρδιαις των πονηρων μαθητων και μαρτυρησουσιν αὐτοις.

IXa

1. Men have hands and feet, but dogs only feet.
2. The lamps are shining in the hands of the daughters.
3. Here laid Philip the father his twelve-year-old son, Nikoteles, his great hope.

   (Note: genitive case expresses age.)
4. Man is the measure of all things.
5. In the Nile are many crocodiles; the Egyptians do not kill them, thinking them sacred. During the winter months (accusative expressing duration of time) the crocodile does not eat anything, and spends most of the day on the land, and the night in the river; for the water is warmer than the air. The crocodile has the eyes of a pig, but big teeth in proportion to its body. It is the only one of the animals which has not a tongue, nor does it move the lower jaw. The others run away from it, but the wagtail is at peace. For the crocodile in the river has its mouth full of leeches, but coming out on the land opens its mouth and the wagtail enters it and eats up the leeches; and the crocodile does not injure it.

   (This passage is slightly modified from Herodotus, the earliest Greek historian.)

IXb

παις ἐστι θαυμαστον ζωον. ὀτε μικρος ἐστι βλεπει ὁραματα ἐλπιδος και γινωσκει ὀτι ποιησει ἀγαθα (not χρηματα because " things " is only general) ἐν τω κοσμω. ὀτε ἐστι μαθητης ἀναγινωσκει τα βιβλια και μανθανει πολλα. οἱ γονεις αὐτου χαιρουσιν ἐν τη σοφια αὐτου, και πιστευουσιν ὀτι ζητησει την δοξαν ἐν τω κοσμω. ἡ λαμπας της ἀληθειας λαμπει ἐν τοις ὀφθαλμοις αὐτου, και τα ὠτα

ἀκουει την φωνην της γνωσεως. ἡγεμων ἐστι του ἀγωνος
και το ὀνομα ἐν τοις στομασι των ἀνθρωπων. ὀτε εὑρισκει
γυναικα καταλειπει τον πατερα και την μητερα και τηρει
αὐτην. φυλασσει την εἰκονα αὐτης ἐν τῃ καρδιᾳ και χαιρει
ἐν τῃ χαριτι αὐτης. ἡ δυναμις του σωματος ἐστιν ἰσχυρα,
ἀλλ᾽ οὐ μενει, και το τελος ἀνθρωπου ἐγγιζει. αἱ τριχες
(not ἡ θριξ, which would mean only one hair!) εἰσι λευκαι,
οὐκ ἐχει ὀδοντας και ἡ φλοξ του πνευματος ἀποθνησκει ἐν
τῳ σκοτει.

Xa. The Governor

The governor was a true gentleman (καλος και ἀγαθος,
or καλος κἀγαθος was the classical Greek definition of a
gentleman). He did not keep his money in his own hands,
but helped the students. His father's mother received five
pieces of silver monthly from the preachers in the city,
and the preachers taught his father freely. Therefore the
governor said that they were the saviours of his father
and honoured them. In the assembly of the people he
witnessed to his faith, and demanded freedom for the
Christians. For five years he governed the province and
all men loved and honoured him. His name was in the
mouths of the common people (lit. the crowd) and his
end filled them with grief.

Xb

οἱ γονεις ἐπεμψαν τον παιδα εἰς την πολιν ὀτι οὐκ ἠν
ἐργον ἐν τῳ ἀμπελωνι. ἐν τῃ χειρι αὐτου ἠν ὀλιγον
ἀργυριον (ὀλιγα χρηματα), και ἐν τῃ καρδιᾳ ἐλπις. περι-
επατησε παρα την ὁδον νυκτος (genitive of " time within
which " a thing happens) και εἰδε (ἐβλεψε) τους ἀστερας
ἐν τοις οὐρανοις. ἐν τῃ πολει ἐζητησε τον οἰκον ἱερεως
και ᾐτησεν βρωμα, ἀλλ᾽ ὁ ἱερευς οὐκ ἐβοηθησεν αὐτῳ. οἱ
κυνες ἐφωνησαν και ἡρπασαν το ἱματιον αὐτου, ἀλλ᾽ ἐτυψε
τα στοματα αὐτων και ἐσιωπησαν. ἐν ἑτερῳ οἰκῳ εἰδε
την φλογα πυρος και λαμπαδα παρα εἰκονι, και ᾐτησεν
ἀρτον και ὑδωρ. ἠκουσε την φωνην γυναικος ἐν τῳ οἰκῳ και
αὐτη εἰπεν τῃ θυγατρι, " δος ἀρτον τῳ παιδι ".

XIa. A Fable of Aesop

A dog which was carrying meat, was crossing a river. When he saw his own shadow in the water he thought that it was another dog and it had the meat (note tenses of original). Therefore he threw away his own meat and snatched that of the other, so that he lost both. For the one did not exist and the other fell into the river.

XIb

ὁ βασιλευς ἠλθεν εἰς ἑτεραν πολιν και κατελιπε τα χρηματα ἐν ταις χερσι των δουλων. ὁ μεν δουλος ἐλαβε δεκα ταλαντα, ὁ δε πεντε, ὁ δε δυο. ὁ βασιλευς ἐμεινε ἐν τη ἑτερᾳ πολει ἐξ μηνας και τοτε ὑπηγαγε προς τον οἰκον. ἐφωνησε (ἐκαλεσε) τους δουλους οἱ ἠλθον και ἠνεγκον τα ταλαντα. ὁ πρωτος δουλος εἰπε, " ἰδου, ἐλαβον δεκα ταλαντα και νυν ἐχω εἰκοσι ". ὁ δευτερος εἰπε, " ἰδου, ἐλαβον πεντε ταλαντα και νυν ἐχω δεκα ". ὁ βασιλευς ἐτιμησε τους ἀγαθους δουλους οἱ ἀνηνεγκον τα χρηματα. ὁ τριτος δουλος εἰπε, " ἐγνων ὁτι ὁ βασιλευς ἐχει πολλα χρηματα, ὡστε ἐφαγον και ἐπιον και νυν οὐδεν ἐχω ". ὁ βασιλευς εἰπε, " πονηρε δουλε, ὁς οὐκ ἐμαθες σοφιαν " και ἐξεβαλεν αὐτον ἐξω της πολεως.

XIIa

It is good for a man to eat and drink because he received his body from God. It is good to seek after wisdom, because the wise man knows the mysteries of the world. If you wish to know the truth you must ask God to help you (lit. " it is necessary you to ask "—note this construction very carefully, and do not try to make a personal verb—it is impersonal, and never has a personal subject, but always the accusative and infinitive). Man is not able to find righteousness in the world. He wishes to do good but does not wish to keep the commandments of God. He wishes to know the truth but does not wish to leave his own thoughts and to do the will of God. The will of God is good, and to do it is life for men (dative expresses

person for whom it is an advantage). Sin remains in men
so that they die. But the love of God saves them, so that
they enter into his kingdom.

XIIb

εἰ θελεις ποιειν ἀγαθον, δει τηρειν τας ἐντολας του θεου
και ἡ πρωτη ἐντολη ἐστι φιλειν τους ἀνθρωπους. ὁ ᾿Ιησους
εἰπεν παραβολην περι ἀγαπης. εἰπεν ὁτι φιλειν ἀνθρωπους
ἐστι βοηθησαι αὐτοις. ὁ ἱερευς και ὁ Λευϊτης οὐκ ἠθελησαν
βοηθησαι τω ἀνθρωπω, ἀλλα ὁ Σαμαρειτης ἠνεγκεν αὐτον
προς το πανδοχειον και εἰπε τω πανδοχει θεραπευειν αὐτον.
το θελημα του Σαμαρειτου ἠν ἀγαθον ποιειν τω ἀνθρωπω
και οὑτως ἐτηρησε τας ἐντολας του θεου.

XIIIa

There was a man in Babylon and his name was Joachim.
And he took a wife whose name was Susanna, the daughter
of Hilkiah, beautiful and reverencing the Lord. And her
parents were righteous and taught their daughter according to the law of Moses. And two elders, coming into
the house of Joachim and seeing his wife walking in her
husband's garden, and desiring her, turned their eyes to
do evil. And the woman came into the garden and the
two elders were looking at her.

(Note the sentences beginning with και which is an
import from the Hebrew original.)

XIIIb

οἱ πονηροι πρεσβυτεροι ἐλθοντες εἰς την ἐκκλησιαν εἰπον
ὁτι ἡ γυνη ἠν λεγουσα μετα νεανιου, αὐτοι δε ἐκβαλοντες
αὐτον ἐκ του παραδεισου ἐκρατησαν αὐτην. ἀκουων τους
λογους των πρεσβυτερων ὁ λαος κατεκρινε την Σουσανναν
ἀποθανειν, ὁ δε Δανιηλ ἀναπηδησας ἐβοησε, " ἐγω εἰμι
ἀθωος του αἱματος της γυναικος ". τοτε ἐκελευσε τον
πρωτον πρεσβυτερον λεγειν ὁπου ἡ γυνη ἠν λαλουσα μετα
του νεανιου, και εἰπεν, " ὑπο συκη ". τοτε ἠρωτησε τον
δευτερον πρεσβυτερον, και εἰπεν αὐτω " ὑπο ἐλαια ". ὁ δε

Δανιηλ ἀκουσας εἰπεν " οἱ δυο πρεσβυτεροι λεγουσι ψευδη ",
και οὑτως ἐσωσε την γυναικα.

XIVa

1. Jesus says to him, " Because you have seen me, have you believed? Blessed are those who did not see and believed ".
2. Now that I have become a man I have put away childish things.
3. I have not injured the Jews, as you well know.
4. Temptation has not seized you except on a human scale.
5. For God has spoken through the mouth of the prophets.
6. He brought Greeks into the temple and has defiled the holy place.
7. And going away to the house she saw the devil gone out of the child.
8. The kingdom of heaven has come near.
9. What I have written, I have written.
10. Lord, in thee have we trusted.

XIVb

1. καλως μεμαθηκα τους λογους.
2. ὁτε γεγονας ἀνηρ, δει σε διδαξαι τους ἀλλους.
3. ὁ κυριος εἰρηκε κακα περι σου.
4. εἰρηκα ὑμιν τους λογους της ἀληθειας ἀλλα ὑμεις οὐ πεπιστευκατε.
5. ὁ ἑωρακαμεν και ἀκηκοαμεν, ἀπαγγελλομεν ὑμιν.
6. το δαιμονιον (πονηρον πνευμα) εἰληφε τον παιδα.
7. πεπληρωκατε την Ἰερουσαλημ (indeclinable) της διδαχης ὑμων (verbs of filling are followed by genitive of the object concerned).
8. ὁ διδασκαλος ἐληλυθε και δει τους μαθητας ἀκουσαι αὐτον.

XVa

For ten years the Greeks fought about Troy, and Agamemnon and Achilles, who were leaders of the Greeks,

differed about a girl. How this happened you shall immediately hear. Chryses, the priest of Apollo, wished to get
back his girl, whom Agamemnon took, but Agamemnon
did not accept his gifts and said, "We Greeks do not
fight for nothing; if we win a girl, we do not send her
back". So Apollo was angry with the Greeks, so that
he came by night and destroyed many. Calchas the
prophet said, "You, Agamemnon, did not accept the
gifts, nor release the daughter of the priest. If you will
send her back, all will be well". Therefore Agamemnon
said, "I will send back the girl and will take Briseis,
Achilles' girl". So, according to Homer, began the wrath
of Achilles.

XVb

ὅτε οἱ ἀπόστολοι ἤρξαντο εὐαγγελίζεσθαι τους Ἕλληνας,
αὐτοι ἐδεξαντο μετα χαρας. ὁ Παυλος ἐλθων προς Ἀθηνας
ἐλαλησε τοις σοφοις ἐν τῳ Ἀρειοπαγῳ. τοτε ἠλθεν προς
Κορινθον και εἰργασατο μετα Ἀκυλου. ἡ πολις της
Κορινθου ἠν πονηρα ἀλλα πολλοι των Κορινθιων ἐπιστευ-
σαν. ὁ Παυλος ἐδυνατο πειθειν αὐτους ἀκολουθειν τῳ
κυριῳ, και ὑπηκουον τοις λογοις αὐτου. ἐνεδυσαντο το
πνευμα της δικαιοσυνης και ἐβαπτισαντο ἐν τῳ ὀνοματι
του κυριου.

XVIa

There was once a man who was sent by the king into
another city, and as he was going along the road he was
seized by robbers. The man was angry and said, "I am
the king's messenger, and you will be pursued and punished
by the king". The robbers, hearing this, were afraid and
began to discuss with one another. One said "The king
will come and seize us and we shall be thrown into prison".
But the other said in reply (lit. "answering said"), "We
shall release the messenger and run away, so that we shall
not be caught". But the leader said, "Why are you dis-
cussing amongst yourselves? When the messenger is dead

he will not be able to report the matter to the king, and a corpse which has been hidden will not be found ".

XVIb

ὅτε οἱ μαθηται συνηλθον ἐν τη Πεντηκοστη ἡμερᾳ, ἡχος ἡκουσθη ὡς βιαιου πνευματος, και ὁλος ὁ οἰκος οὐ ἠσαν καθημενοι ἐπληρωθη. και ὠφθησαν γλωσσαι ὡς πυρος και ἐπληρωθησαν πνευματος ἁγιου, και ἠρξαντο λαλειν ἑτεραις γλωσσαις. οἱ λογοι ἡκουσθησαν ὑπο του λαου και ἐφοβηθησαν ὅτι εἰδον το τερας (note: although λαος is singular the following verbs may be general plural as in English, since λαος is not the grammatical subject). τοτε ὁ Πετρος ἀποκριθεις εἰπεν αὐτοις, " τουτο ἐγενετο τη δυναμει του θεου. ὁ Ἰησους ὁ Ναζωραιος ἐσταυρωθη ὑφ' ὑμων, ἀλλα ὑψωθη (augment absorbed in v) ὑπο του θεου, και ἐν τῳ ὀνοματι αὐτου το Ἁγιον Πνευμα ἐληλυθε ".

XVIIa

Jesus said to his disciples, " Let us go elsewhere, into the other villages, so that I may preach there also. Whoever receives me, receives my Father. For the Son of Man did not come to judge the world but that the world might be saved through him. But the world will never believe on me until I come on the clouds of heaven ". The disciples said in reply, " Lord, what shall we do? If the crowds do not hear your words, how will they hear ours? " Jesus said, " Wherever you preach the gospel, do not be afraid that men will kill you, for I am with you for ever " (lit. " to the age ").

XVIIb

ὁ Παυλος ἐγραψεν ἐν τη ἐπιστολη, τι οὐν ποιησωμεν ; μενωμεν ἐν ἁμαρτιᾳ, ἱνα ἡ χαρις περισσευη ; ἀλλ' ὁς ἀν βλεψη την ἀγαπην του θεου οὐ δυναται ἁμαρτειν, και ὁς ἀν ἁμαρτη οὐ μη εἰσελθη εἰς την βασιλειαν των οὐρανων. ὁ Ἰησους ἠλθεν ἱνα ἐχωμεν ζωην, και ἱνα βοηθωμεν ἀλληλοις. τηρωμεν τας ἐντολας αὐτου ἑως ἀν ἰδωμεν αὐτον ἐν τη

δοξῃ αὐτου. ἡ ἐλπις ἡμων ἐστιν ἐν αὐτῳ ὡστε μη φοβη-
θηναι μη.καταλιπῃ ἡμας. ὁταν εἰσελθωμεν εἰς πειρασμον
δυναμεθα εἰπειν αὐτῳ, κυριε, μη ἀποστρεψῃς ἀπο του λαου
σου.

XVIIIa

In the world it is clear that if anyone shouts he is
honoured; but if anyone humbles himself, his glory is not
manifested. A doctor treats and heals the poor, but no
one loves him. But if he seeks the opinion of men and
exalts his own wisdom, all men honour him and his house
is filled. Do you not see that those who speak many words
are called wise? Let us be glad therefore, and filled with
joy that in heaven those who have been humbled will be
exalted, and those who exalted themselves will be humbled.
Man is not justified by his own wisdom, but by the love
of God. The gospel witnesses that Jesus was crucified so
that men might be justified, and so that in the last day
he might save those who love him.

XVIIIb

ὁ Ἰησους εἰπεν, ἐαν ἀγαπατε με, τηρησετε τας ἐντολας
μου. ἀλλ᾽ εἰ θεωρουμεν τον κοσμον, ὁρωμεν ὁτι οἱ ἀνθρωποι
οὐ ποιουσι τουτο. ἐπιθυμουσι της σωτηριας, ἀλλ᾽ οὐ
θελουσι ταπεινουν ἑαυτους (ταπεινουσθαι). πεπληρωμενοι
εἰσι της πονηριας και λατρευουσι τα εἰδωλα. αἰτησωμεν,
τις δικαιουται τοις ἐργοις αὐτου ; αἱ γραφαι μαρτυρουσιν
ὁτι οὐδεις ἐστι δικαιος. δει τον ἀνθρωπον σιωπαν ὁτε ὁ
θεος λαλει ἱνα φανεροι την ἀληθειαν αὐτου. ὁτε γενναται
εἰς τον κοσμον ἐᾳ την ἁμαρτιαν κρατησαι αὐτον και ἀγαπᾳ
την ἰδιαν δοξαν, και ὑψοι ἑαυτον. αἰτωμεν τον θεον ἰασθαι
την ἁμαρτιαν ἡμων και φανερουν την δοξαν αὐτου ἐν ἡμιν
ἱνα ἀγαλλιωμεθα ἐν τῃ ἡμερᾳ του κυριου.

XIXa

A householder wished to go into another city and standing his servants in front of him he gave to them money

157

in order that they might work until he came. The servants stood and said to one another " What shall we do? " One said, " Let us buy sheep, so that we may sell the lambs and get money " But the other standing by the side said, " I will put my money in the bank, so that I may not lose it ". The householder came and told them to render account. The one received five pieces of silver and deposited with his master ten; and the master said, " You have done well, I will set you up as ruler of the household ". The other received two pieces of silver and repaid the two, and the master said in anger, " I know that you are a bad servant ", and handed him over to the officers, so that he should be thrown into prison.

XIXb

ὁ Κύριος εἶπεν, ὅς ἂν ἔχῃ, αὐτῷ δοθησεται. εἰ θελομεν δεχεσθαι τὴν χαριν αὐτου δει ἡμας δουναι αὐτῷ τὴν ἀγαπην ἡμων. ἔθηκεν ἡμας ἐν τῳ κοσμῳ ἱνα ποιησωμεν τα ἐργα αὐτου, και ἐαν ποιωμεν το θελημα αὐτου ἀναστησει ἡμας ἐν τῃ ἐσχατῃ ἡμερᾳ. οἱδεν ὁτι ἐσμεν ἁμαρτωλοι, ἀλλ᾽ ἀφησει τα ἁμαρτηματα ἡμων και παραστησει ἡμας ἐνωπιον του πατρος ὡς ἁγιους. δωμεν αὐτῳ τὴν ἀγαπην ἡμων ἱνα εἰδωμεν το θελημα αὐτου και ποιησωμεν αὐτο. οὐχ ὡς Ἰουδας προεδωκεν αὐτον τοις ἀρχιερευσι και ἀπεδοτο τον δεσποτην αὐτου, ἀλλ᾽ ὡς οἱ μαρτυρες ἐθηκαν τας ψυχας ὑπερ αὐτου. λαβωμεν το πανοπλιον του θεου ἱνα στωμεν ἐν τῃ πονηρᾳ ἡμερᾳ και μη ἀποσταθωμεν ἀπ᾽ αὐτου.

XXa

Now I shall give you commands, you observe them.
Students, stand up—sit down.
First student, give me the book—take it.
Second student, write your name.
Third student, lift your hand—put it on the table.
Fourth and fifth students, go out of the room.
Sixth student, bring them into the room.

Seventh student, tell them to sit down.
Eighth student, touch your face.
Ninth student, stop sitting down, stand up.
Tenth student, tell him to sit down.

XXb

ἐγείρεσθε πρωΐ.
λούσασθε ὕδατι.
μη μενετε ἐν τῃ κλινῃ μακρον χρονον.
ἀκουετε τον διδασκαλον και μη κοιμηθητε ἐν τῃ σχολῃ.
γραψατε τους σοφους λογους του διδασκαλου.
ἀποκρινασθε προς τα ἐρωτηματα του διδασκαλου ταχεως.
ἀναγινωσκετε τα βιβλια και τηρειτε τους λογους αὐτων
ἐν ταις καρδιαις ὑμων.
μη παυεσθε εὐχεσθαι.

Examples from Greek poets in Lesson XX

1. All are kinsmen of the prosperous.
2. He who is ignorant of letters looks but does not see.
3. The wise learn many things from their enemies.
4. Evil communications corrupt good manners.
      (But it is not certain whether Paul intended it to be
      poetry or not!)
5. If God is willing, all things become possible.
      (This is a genitive absolute—see Lesson XXVI.)
6. For somehow there is this disease in tyranny—not to
   trust one's friends.
7. The body is mortal, but the soul immortal.

XXIa

Everyone says that man must do good, but everyone
does not do it.   Their word is true, but their actions false.
For man is foolish and full of all kinds of injustice.   Although he wishes to do good he practises evil, and his will
is weak.   Those who love the true love something great,
but it is impossible always to speak the truth.

XXIb

ἡ ἀγαπη ἐστι μεγαλη και ἀγαθη, και οἱ ζητουντες την ἀγαπην εὑρησουσι την ἀληθη χαραν. οἱ ἀφρονες εἰσι πληρεις της ἀδικιας, και οὐ ζητουσιν ἀγαθα. παντες αὑτοι λεγουσι ψευδη, και τα ἐργα παντα πονηρα. εἰ ἀνθρωπος θελει λεγειν τα ἀληθη και ποιειν τα ἀγαθα εὑρισκει πολλην χαραν. ἀλλα οἱ ἀνθρωποι εἰσιν ἀσθενεις και ἀπειροι της δικαιοσυνης. πολλοι θελουσι ποιειν μεγαλα ἐν τῳ κοσμῳ και λαβειν ζωην αἰωνιον, ἀλλα πλανωνται. ἀδυνατον ἐστιν ἀνθρωπον ἀσθενη ποιησαι το ἀληθες τῃ δε χαριτι του θεου παντα δυνατα.

XXIIa

1. It is better to be silent than to speak in vain.
2. No law is stronger than necessity.
3. Second thoughts are somehow wiser.
4. He who does most, sins most, amongst mortal men.
5. There is one man worse, another better, for the same work; but no one of men is himself wise for all things.
6. There was an oracle of Apollo in Delphi:
      Sophocles is wise, Euripides wiser
      But of all men the wisest is Socrates.
7. Half is more than the whole, as Hesiod says.
8. Water is best, as Pindar says.
9. The last error shall be worse than the first.
10. Be a slave freely—you will not be a slave.

XXIIb

ἀληθως ἡ ἀγαπη ἐστι το μεγιστον δωρον του θεου ἀνθρω-
ποις. ἡ σοφια ἀγαθη ἀλλ᾽ ἡ ἀγαπη κρεισσων. ὁ φιλων ἰσχυροτερος ἐστι του ἐχθρου (ἡ ὁ ἐχθρος), ὁτι μαλιστα δυναται ἀφιεναι τας ἁμαρτιας. το ἀγαπαν μειζον ἐστι του φιλειν (see Lesson XXV). ὁ φιλος ζητει το ἀγαθον του φιλου, ὁ δε ἀγαπων τιθησι την ψυχην ὑπερ του ἀγαπητου. ἡ ἀγαπη του Χριστου μειζων ἐστι της ἀγαπης ἀδελφου, και ἡ ἀγαπη του Θεου μειζων ἐστι της ἀγαπης πατρος. οἱ εὑρισ-
κοντες αὐτην εὑρισκουσι χαραν και εὑρισκουσι περισσοτερον.

XXIIIa

1. Who knows whether to live is to die, and to die is reckoned below as living?
2. To love God with one's whole heart and to love one's neighbour as oneself is more than all burnt-offerings and sacrifices.
3. Before some came from James, Peter was eating with the Gentiles.
4. After they became silent James answered.
5. You have not, because you do not ask.
6. Jesus came into the world in order that sinners might be saved.
7. Lord, come down, before my child dies.

XXIIIb

πρo τoυ ἐλθειν εἰς την πoλιν δει αἰτεισθαι (ἐρωταν) περι της ὁδoυ. μετα τo ἀκoυσαι σε τoυτo, δυνησει ὁδoν πoιειν ἐκει, ἀλλα ἐν τω πoρευεσθαι μη λαλησῃς μηδενι. ἐαν τις λεγῃ σoι εἰσελθειν εἰς τoν oἰκoν αὐτoυ μη ἀκoυσῃς αὐτoυ. κλεψει τo ἀργυριoν σoυ ὡστε μη δυνασθαι σε ἀγoρασαι ἀρτoν. πρo τoυ αὐτoν ἀρπαζειν σε φυγε. ὁ σoφoς oὐ πιστευει τoις μωρoις (ἀφρoσιν) oἱ λεγoυσι πoλυ ἀργυριoν εἰναι ἐν τῃ πoλει δια τo γνωναι ὁτι αὐτoι εἰσι μωρoι (ἀφρoνες). πρoς τo λαβειν ἀργυριoν, δει ἀνθρωπoν ἐργαζεσθαι, δια τo εἰρηκεναι τoν θεoν τω Ἀδαμ ὁτι ἐν τω ἐργαζεσθαι δει φαγειν.

XXIVa

And as he was going along by the sea of Galilee he saw Simon and Andrew, Simon's brother, casting nets in the sea. And he said to them, "Come after me". And leaving their nets they went after Jesus. And as they were going along, John and James, the sons of Zebedee, were in the boat. Jesus called them as they were mending their nets. When their father Zebedee saw Jesus he released them and said, "I am not the one to prevent you, if you wish to go with him ". And after Jesus had gone into the synagogue he began to teach, and he was teaching them as one having authority. And when a man with an unclean spirit came, the Pharisees said, " What will he do? " But Jesus knew their discussions and said in reply, " Why are you questioning amongst yourselves, saying, ' What will he do? ' Whilst I am in the world I must work the works of my Father." And he said to the man, " Get up and come to me ". And as Jesus said " Come out of him ", the demon convulsed him and came out.

XXIVb

ὁ Σαυλος ἐλθων προς τον ἀρχιερεα ᾐτησατο ἀπ' αὐτου ἐπιστολας προς Δαμασκον. ἠθελησε γαρ ἐξελθων ἐκει και εὑρων τους ὀντας της ὁδου ἀναγαγειν αὐτους δεδεμενους προς Ἱερουσαλημ. και ἐγγιζοντος αὐτου προς Δαμασκον ἐξαιφνης αὐτον περιηστραψεν φως ἐκ του οὐρανου. και ἠκουσεν φωνην λεγουσαν αὐτῳ, Σαουλ, Σαουλ, τι με διωκεις ; οἱ ὀντες μετ' αὐτου ἀκουοντες την φωνην ἐφοβηθησαν, και μη βλεποντες μηδενα εἰπον ὁτι ἀγγελος μετ' αὐτου λαλει. ὁ δε Σαυλος ἀκουσας την φωνην ἐπεσεν ἐπι την γην, και των ὀφθαλμων ἀνεῳγμενων οὐδενα ἐβλεψεν. τοτε μαθητης τις, ὀνοματι Ἀνανιας, ἀκουσας ἀγγελιαν ἀπο του κυριου, ἀναστας ἠλθεν προς τον οἰκον οὑ ὁ Σαυλος ἐμενε. του δε Σαυλου προσευχομενου, ὁ Ἀνανιας ἐλθων προς τον οἰκον εἰσηλθεν. και ἐπιθεις τας χειρας τῳ Σαυλῳ εἰπεν, ὁ Ἰησους ὁ φανεις σοι ἐν τῃ ὁδῳ ἀπεστειλε με ἀνοιξαι τους ὀφθαλμους σου. και ἐπιθεντος αὐτου τας χειρας τῳ Σαυλῳ οἱ ὀφθαλμοι αὐτου ἀνεῳχθησαν και ἀνεβλεψεν.

XXVa

1. If I spoke wrongly, immediately I repented.
2. If you are the son of God, come down from the cross.
   (Imperative for indicative in present simple condition.)

3. If the dead are not raised, neither is Christ risen.
(A clear indication that the primary reference of the perfect is to the present state.)
4. If you wish to enter into life, keep the commandments.
5. If the salt is spoiled, with what shall it be salted?
6. If you forgive men their faults, your heavenly Father will forgive you also.
(*Note:* καὶ emphasizes ὑμῖν.)
7. If this plan is of men, it will be destroyed.
8. If the householder had known in what watch the thief was coming, he would have stayed awake.
(Pluperfect for aorist in protasis.)
9. Lord, if you had been here, my brother would not have died.
(Commentators produce all kinds of weird and wonderful explanations about why in a large number of places, of which this is a sample, the imperfect of εἰμί is found where an aorist would have been expected. Few seem to note the obvious point—there is no aorist of εἰμί.)
10. (*a*) If you had known me, you would have known my Father also.
(*b*) If you knew me, you would know my Father also.
(The tense in both parts is a pluperfect, but οἶδα is a defective verb, and the pluperfect is therefore usually equivalent to an imperfect. In sentence 8, however, the same tense is equivalent to an aorist, so it is grammatically possible to take it as either a past unfulfilled condition, or a present unfulfilled condition. You must decide from the context, but since here it is isolated, no decision is possible.)
11. If you were blind, you would not háve sin.
12. If God were your father, you would love me.

XXVb

1. εἰ ἡ βασιλεια των οὐρανων ἦν ἐντος ὑμων, ᾔδειτε ἀν την εἰρηνην του θεου ἐν ταις καρδιαις.

2. εἰ ἐποιησαμεν ταυτα, οὐκ ἀν ἠμεν ἀληθεις δουλοι του θεου.

(See note on sentence 9 above.)

3. ἐαν ὁ οἰκοδεσποτης εἰδῃ ποιᾳ φυλακῃ ὁ κλεπτης ἐρχεται, γρηγορησει.

4. ἐαν ἀγαπατε με, τηρησετε τας ἐντολας μου.

5. εἰ μη ὁ Ἰησους ἠλθεν προς την Ἰερουσαλημ, οὐκ ἀν ἐσταυρωθη.

6. εἰ μη ἡ δικαιοσυνη ὑμων πλεων ἐστι ἠ των Φαρισαιων, οὐ μη δυνηθητε σωθηναι.

7. εἰ ᾐδεις το δωρον του θεου και τις ἐστιν ὁ αἰτουμενος ὑδωρ, ᾐτεις ἀν αὐτον και ἐδιδου ἀν σοι ὑδωρ ζων.

8. εἰ τι ἠδικησα, εἰπε μοι και μετανοησω.

9. εἰ ἀνθρωποις ἀρεσκω, οὐκ εἰμι δουλος Χριστου.

10. εἰ ἀληθως ἠσθα δικαιος, ᾐδεις ἀν τουτο εἰναι ἁμαρτημα.

GREEK—ENGLISH VOCABULARY

ἀγαθος—good
ἀγαλλιαομαι—I rejoice greatly
ἀγαπαω—I love
ἀγαπη, -ης (f.)—love
ἀγαπητος—beloved
ἀγγελλω—I announce
ἀγγελος, -ου (m.)—messenger
ἁγιος—holy
ἀγρος, -ου (m.)—field
ἀγω—I lead
ἀγων, -ωνος (m.)—contest, game
ἀδελφος, -ου (m.)—brother
ἀδικεω—I injure
ἀδυνατος—impossible
ἀει—always
ἀθανατος—immortal
ἀθῳος—innocent
αἰθηρ, -ερος (m.)—air
αἱμα, -ατος (n.)—blood
αἰρω—I lift
αἰτεω—I ask
αἰτια, -ας (f.)—cause
αἰων, -ωνος (m.)—age
αἰωνιος—eternal
ἀκουω—I hear
ἀκριβης—careful
ἀκριβως—carefully
ἁλας, -ατος (n.)—salt
ἀληθεια, -ας (f.)—truth
ἀληθης—true
ἁλιζω—I salt
ἀλλα—but
ἀλλαχου—elsewhere
ἀλληλους—one another
ἀλλος—other
ἁμαρτανω—I sin
ἁμαρτημα, -ατος (n.)—sin
ἁμαρτια, -ας (f.)—sin
ἁμαρτωλος, -ου (m.)—sinner
ἀμνος, -ου (m.)—lamb
ἀμπελων, -ωνος (m.)—vineyard

ἀμφιβαλλω—cast (nets)
ἀμφοτεροι—both
ἀναγγελλω—I announce
ἀναγινωσκω—I read
ἀναγκη, -ης (f.)—necessity
ἀναπηδαω—I jump up
ἀναστασις, -εως (f.)—resurrection
ἀναφερω—I bring back
ἀνεμος, -ου (m.)—wind
ἀνηρ, ἀνδρος (m.)—man
ἀνθρωπος, -ου (m.)—man
ἀνθρωπινος—human
ἀνοιγω—I open
ἀξιος—worthy
ἀπειρος—unskilled
ἀπο—from
ἀποθνησκω—I die
ἀποκρινομαι—I answer
ἀποκτεινω—I kill
ἀποστελλω—I send
ἀποστολος, -ου (m.)—apostle
ἀποστρεφω—I turn away
ἁπτομαι—I touch
ἀπωλεια, -ας (f.)—destruction
ἀργος—lazy
ἀργυριον, -ου (n.)—silver, money
ἀριστερος—left (hand)
ἀριστος—best
ἁρπαζω—I snatch, seize
ἀρτος, -ου (m.)—bread
ἀρχιερευς, -εως (m.)—high priest
ἀρχη, -ης (f.)—beginning, rule
ἀρχομαι—I begin
ἀρχων, -οντος (m.)—ruler
ἀσθενης—weak
ἀσπαζομαι—I greet
ἀστηρ, -ερος (m.)—star
αὑτη—this (fem.)
αὐτος—he
ἀφεσις, -εως (f.)—forgiveness

165

ἀφιημι—I forgive
ἀφρων—foolish

βαινω—I go
βαλλω—I throw
βαπτισμα, -ατος (n.)—baptism
βαπτιστης, -ου (m.)—Baptist
βαπτω—I dip
βασιλεια, -ας (f.)—kingdom
βασιλευς, -εως (m.)—king
βιβλιον, -ου (n.)—book
βιος, -ου (m.)—life
βλαπτω—I injure
βλεπω—I see
βοαω—I call out
βοηθεω—I help
βουλη, -ης (f.)—counsel, plan
βουλομαι—I wish
βους, βοος (m.)—ox
βροτος, -ου (m.)—mortal man
βρωμα, -ατος (n.)—food

γαρ—for, because
γενεα, -ας (f.)—generation
γενναομαι—I am born
γενος, -ους (n.)—race, nation
γη, γης (f.)—earth, land
γινομαι—I become
γινωσκω—I know
γλωσσα, -ης (f.)—tongue
γναθος, -ου (f.)—jaw
γνωσις, -εως (f.)—knowledge
γονευς, -εως (m.)—parent
γραμμα, -ατος (n.)—letter (of alphabet)
γραμματευς, -εως (m.)—scribe
γραφη, -ης (f.)—writing (pl.— the Scriptures)
γραφω—I write
γρηγορεω—I keep awake
γυνη, γυναικος (f.)—woman, wife

δαιμονιον, -ου (n.)—demon
δε—but
δει—it is necessary
δεισιδαιμων—religious

δεκα—ten
δεκατος—tenth
δενδρον, -ου (n.)—tree
δεξιος—right (hand)
δεομαι—I pray, beseech
δεσποτης, -ου (m.)—master
δευτερος—second
δεχομαι—I receive
δηλον—clear
δημος, -ου (m.)—people
διαβαινω—I cross over
διαβολος, -ου (m.)—devil
διαθηκη, -ης (f.)—covenant, testament
διαλεγομαι—I discuss
διατριβω—I spend (time)
διαφερομαι—I differ
διδασκαλος, -ου (m.)—teacher
διδασκω—I teach
διδωμι—I give
δικαιος—just, righteous
δικαιοσυνη, -ης (f.)—righteousness
δικαιοω—I justify
δικτυον, -ου (n.)—net
διωκω—I pursue
δοξα, -ης (f.)—glory, opinion
δουλος, -ου (m.)—slave, servant
δυναμαι—I am able, I can
δυναμις, -εως (f.)—power
δυνατος—able, possible
δυο—two
δυσεντερια—dysentery
δωδεκα—twelve
δωρεαν—freely
δωρον, -ου (n.)—gift

ἐαω—I allow
ἑβδομος—seventh
ἐγγιζω—I draw near
ἐγγυς—near
ἐγειρω—I rouse
ἐγω—I
ἐθνος, -ους (n.)—tribe, nation
εἰ—if
εἰδωλον, -ου (n.)—idol, image

166

εἴκοσι—twenty
εἴκων, -ονος (f.)—image, picture
εἰρηνη, -ης (f.)—peace
εἰς—into
εἰσαγω—I lead into
ἐκ, ἐξ—out of
ἐκαστος—each
ἐκκλησια, -ας (f.)—assembly,
   church
ἐκκλινω—I bend
ἐκτος—sixth
ἐλεεω—I have mercy on
ἐλευθερια, -ας (f.)—freedom
ἐλευθερος—free
ἐλπις, -ιδος (f.)—hope
ἐμβαινω—I enter
ἐν—in, on
ἐνατος—ninth
ἐνδυω—I put on
ἐνθαδε—here
ἐντολη, -ης (f.)—commandment
ἐνωπιον—in front of, before
ἐξ—six
ἐξουσια, -ας (f.)—authority
ἐπαγγελια, -ας (f.)—promise
ἐπαρχια, -ας (f.)—province
ἐπι—on
ἐπιθυμια, -ας (f.)—desire
ἐπικαλεω—I name
ἐπιστολη, -ης (f.)—letter, epistle
ἐργαζομαι—I work
ἐργατης, -ου (m.)—workman
ἐργον, -ου (n.)—work
ἐρημος, -ου (f.)—desert
ἐρις, -ιδος (f.)—strife
ἐρχομαι—I come, go
ἐρωταω—I ask (question)
ἐσθιω—I eat
ἐστι—it is
ἐσχατος—last
ἑτερος—other
ἐτος, -ους (n.)—year
εὐ—well
εὐαγγελιζομαι—I preach the gospel
εὐαγγελιον, -ου (n.)—gospel

εὐαγγελιστης, -ου (m.)—preacher,
   evangelist
εὐθυς—immediately
εὑρισκω—I find
εὐσεβεω—I reverence
εὐτυχεω—I prosper
ἐχθρος, -ου (m.)—enemy
ἐχω—I have

ζηλωτης, -ου (m.)—jealous person
ζητεω—I seek
ζωη, -ης (f.)—life
ζωνη, -ης (f.)—belt
ζῳον, -ου (n.)—animal

ἡγεμονευω—I govern
ἡγεμων, -ονος (m.)—leader, governor
ἠθος, -ους (n.)—manners, custom
ἡμεις—we
ἡμερα, -ας (f.)—day
ἡμισυ—half
Ἡρωδης, -ου (m.)—Herod
ἠχος, -ους (n.)—sound

θαλασσα, -ης (f.)—sea
θανατος, -ου (m.)—death
θαυμαστος—wonderful
θελημα, -ατος (n.)—will
θελω—I wish, will
θεος, -ου (m.)—god
θεραπευω—I care for
θερμος—warm
θεωρεω—I look at, see
θνητος—mortal
θριξ, τριχος (f.)—hair
θρονος, -ου (m.)—throne
θυγατηρ, -τρος (f.)—daughter
θυρα, -ας (f.)—door
θυσια, -ας (f.)—sacrifice

ἰαομαι—I cure
ἰατρος, -ου (m.)—doctor
ἰδιος—own

167

ἱερευς, -εως (m.)—priest
ἱερον, -ου (n.)—temple
ἱερος—sacred
'Ιησους, -ου (m.)—Jesus
ἱματιον, -ου (n.)—garment
'Ιορδανης, -ου (m.)—Jordan
ἱστημι—I make to stand
ἰσχυρος—strong
ἰσχυω—I am strong, am able
ἰχθυς, -υος (m.)—fish
'Ιωαννης, -ου (m.)—John

καθαρος—pure
καθεδρα, -ας (f.)—seat, chair
καθιζω—I sit
και—and
καινος—new, fresh
καιπερ—although
καιρος, -ου (m.)—time, opportunity
κακος—bad
καλεω—I call
καλος—good, beautiful
καλως—well, beautifully
καρδια, -ας (f.)—heart
καρπος, -ου (m.)—fruit
κατα—according to
καταβαινω—I descend
κατακρινω—I condemn
καταλειπω—I leave, desert
καταλυω—I destroy
καταπινω—I drink up
καταργεω—I cancel
καταρτιζω—I mend
καταστροφη, -ης (f.)—catastrophe
κατω—below, downward
κελευω—I command
κερδος, -ους (n.)—gain
κεφαλη, -ης (f.)—head
κηρυσσω—I preach
κινεω—I move
κλεπτης, -ου (m.)—thief
κλεπτω—I steal
κλινη, -ης (f.)—bed
κοιμαομαι—I go to sleep
κοινοω—I defile

κορη, -ης (f.)—girl
κοσμος, -ου (m.)—world
κραζω—I cry out
κρατεω—I seize, arrest
κρατος, -ους (n.)—strength
κρεας, -ατος (n.)—meat
κριμα, -ατος (n.)—judgement, verdict
κρινω—I judge
κρισις, -εως (f.)—judgement
κριτης, -ου (m.)—judge
κροκοδειλος, -ου (m.)—crocodile
κρυπτος—hidden, secret
κρυπτω—I hide
κυκλος, -ου (m.)—circle
κυριος, -ου (m.)—lord
κυων, κυνος (m.)—dog
κωμη, -ης (f.)—village

λαλεω—I speak, say
λαμβανω—I take, receive
λαμπας, -αδος (f.)—lamp
λαμπω—I shine
λαος, -ου (m.)—people
λατρευω—I serve, worship
λεγω—I say
λευκος—white
λεων, -οντος (m.)—lion
ληστης, -ου (m.)—robber
λογος, -ου (m.)—word
λουω—I wash
λυπη, -ης (f.)—grief
λυω—I loosen

μαθητης, -ου (m.)—student disciple
μακαριος—happy, blessed
μακρος—long
μανθανω—I learn
μαρτυρεω—I witness
ματαιος—vain
ματην—vainly
μαχομαι—I fight
μεγας—great, big
μενω—I remain

μεσος—middle
μετα—after, with
μετανοεω—I repent
μετρον, -ου (n.)—measure
μηδεις—no one
μην, μηνος (m.)—month
μητηρ, μητρος (f.)—mother
μικρος—small, little
μισθος, -ου (m.)—reward
μοιχευω—I commit adultery
μονον—only
μονος—alone
μυστηριον, -ου (n.)—mystery
μωραινω—I spoil
μωρος—foolish

νεανιας, -ου (m.)—young man
νεκρος—dead
νεος—new, young
νεφελη, -ης (f.)—cloud
νηπιος, -ου (m.)—infant
νοημα, -ατος (n.)—thought
νομιζω—I think
νομος, -ου (m.)—law
νοσημα, -ατος (n.)—disease
νυν—now
νυξ, νυκτος (f.)—night

ὀγδοος—eighth
ὁδος, -ου (f.)—way, road
ὀδους, -οντος (m.)—tooth
οἰδα—I know
οἰκεω—I dwell
οἰκοδεσποτης, -ου (m.)—house-holder
οἰκος, -ου (m.)—house
ὀλιγος—little, few
ὁλοκαυτωμα, -ατος (n.)—burnt offering
ὁμιλια, -ας (f.)—relationship, association
ὁμοιος—like
ὁμολογεω—I confess
ὀνομα, -ατος (n.)—name
ὁπου—where
ὁπως—how

ὁραμα, -ατος (n.)—vision
ὁραω—I see
ὀργη, -ης (f.)—anger
ὀργιζομαι—I am angry
ὀρθος—straight, right
ὀρος, -ους (n.)—mountain
ὁς—who
ὁτε—when
ὁτι—that, because
οὐ—not
οὐδεις—no one
οὐρανος, -ου (m.)—heaven
οὐς, ὠτος (n.)—ear
οὑτος—this (mas.)
οὑτως—thus
ὀχλος, -ου (m.)—crowd
ὀφειλω—I owe
ὀφθαλμος, -ου (m.)—eye

παθημα, -ατος (n.)—suffering
παθος, -ους (n.)—suffering
παιδιον, -ου (n.)—child
παιδισκη, -ης (f.)—maidservant
παις, παιδος (m.)—boy, servant
παλαιος—ancient
πανδοχειον, -ου (n.)—inn
πανδοχευς, -εως (m.)—innkeeper
πανοπλιον, -ου (n.)—armour
παρα—alongside
παραβολη, -ης (f.)—parable
παραγγελια, -ας (f.)—command-ment
παραδεισος, -ου (m.)—garden
παραπτωμα, -ατος (n.)—fault
παρθενος, -ου (f.)—girl, maiden
παροικεω—I live with, dwell
πας—every, all
πασχω—I suffer
πατηρ, πατρος (m.)—father
παυω—I stop
πειθω—I persuade
πειρασμος, -ου (m.)—trial, temp-tation
πεμπτος—fifth
πεμπω—I send
πεντε—five

169

πεντηκοστος—fiftieth
περι—about, around
περιπατεω—I walk about
περισσευω—I abound
περισσον—abundantly
πηρα, -ας (f.)—bag
πινω—I drink
πιπτω—I fall
πιστευω—I believe
πιστις, -εως (f.)—faith
πιστος—faithful
πλαναω—I deceive
πλανη, -ης (f.)—error
πληθος, -ους (n.)—crowd
πληρης—full
πληροω—I fill
πλησιον—near
   (ὁ πλησιον—neighbour)
πλοιον, -ου (n.)—ship, boat
πνευμα, -ατος (n.)—wind, spirit
ποιεω—I do, make
ποιμην, -ενος (m.)—shepherd
ποιος—of what kind?
πολις, -εως (f.)—city
πολιτης, -ου (m.)—citizen
πολυς—much (pl. many)
πονηρος—wicked
πορευομαι—I go, journey
ποταμος, -ου (m.)—river
πους, ποδος (m.)—foot
πρασσω—I do, practise
πρεσβυτερος, -ου (m.)—elder
προβατον, -ου (n.)—sheep
προς—to
προσευχομαι—I pray
προσηλυτης, -ου (m.)—stranger,
   proselyte
προσκυνεω—I worship
προσωπον, -ου (n.)—face
προφητης, -ου (m.)—prophet
πρωϊ—early in the morning
πρωτος—first
πτωχος—poor
πυρ, πυρος (n.)—fire
πως—how

ῥημα, -ατος (n.)—word

σαββατον, -ου (n.)—Sabbath
σαλπιγξ, -ιγγος (f.)—trumpet
σαρξ, σαρκος (f.)—flesh
σημειον, -ου (n.)—sign, miracle
σιγαω ⎫—⎧I become silent
σιωπαω ⎭ ⎩I remain silent
σκια, -ας (f.)—shadow
σκηνη, -ης (f.)—tent
σκοτος, -ους (n.)—darkness
σοφια, -ας (f.)—wisdom
σοφος—wise
σπειρω—I sow
σπερμα, -ατος (n.)—seed
σταυροω—I crucify
σταχυς, -νος (m.)—ear (of corn)
στομα, -ατος (n.)—mouth
στρατιωτης, -ου (m.)—soldier
στρεφω—I turn
συ—you (sing.)
συγγενης—akin, kinsman
συναγωγη, -ης (f.)—synagogue
συνερχομαι—I come together
συνιημι—I understand
σχισμα, -ατος (n.)—division
σχολη, -ης (f.)—leisure, school
σωζω—I save
σωμα, -ατος (n.)—body
σωτηρ, -ηρος (m.)—saviour
σωτηρια, -ας (f.)—salvation

ταλαντον, -ου (n.)—talent
ταπεινοω—I humble
ταχεως, ταχυ—quickly
τεκνον, -ου (n.)—child
τελεω—I complete
τελος, -ους (n.)—end
τελωνης, -ου (m.)—tax-collector
τερας, -ατος (n.)—wonder,
   miracle
τεταρτος—fourth
τεχνη, -ης (f.)—art, skill
τηρεω—I watch, keep
τι;—what?
τιθημι—I place

τικτω—I bring forth (child)
τιμαω—I honour
τιμωρεω—I punish
τις;—who?
τις—someone, anyone
τοπος, -ου (m.)—place
τοτε—then
τουτο—this (neut.)
τραπεζα, -ης (f.)—table
τριτος—third
τυπτω—I strike
τυραννις, -ιδος (f.)—absolute rule, tyranny
τυραννος, -ου (m.)—absolute ruler, tyrant

ὑδωρ, ὑδατος (n.)—water
υἱος, -ου (m.)—son
ὑμεις—you (pl.)
ὑμνος, -ου (m.)—hymn
ὑπαγω—I return
ὑπακουω—I obey
ὑπαρχει—it exists, it is
ὑπηρετης, -ου (m.)—attendant, officer
ὑπο—under, by
ὑποζυγιον, -ου (n.)—yoke-animal
ὑποκριτης, -ου (m.)—play-actor, hypocrite
ὑπολαμβανω—I think, conjecture
ὑς, ὑος (m.)—pig
ὑψοω—I lift up, exalt

φανερος—clear, manifest
φανεροω—I make clear
φερω—I carry
φευγω—I flee
φημι—I say
φθειρω—I destroy
φιλεω—I love
φιλος, -ου (m.)—friend
φλοξ, φλογος (f.)—flame

φοβεω—I terrify
   (φοβεομαι—I fear)
φοβος, -ου (m.)—fear
φονευω—I murder
φονος, -ου (m.)—murder
φροντις, -ιδος (f.)—thought, anxiety
φυλακη, -ης (f.)—prison
φυλαξ, -ακος (m.)—guard
φυλασσω—I guard
φυλλον, -ου (n.)—leaf
φωνεω—I call
φωνη, -ης (f.)—voice, sound
φως, φωτος (n.)—light

χαιρω—I rejoice
χαρα, -ας (f.)—joy
χαρακτηρ, -ηρος (m.)—character, letter (of alphabet)
χαρις, -ιτος (f.)—grace
χειμων, -ωνος (m.)—winter
χειρ, χειρος (f.)—hand
χιτων, -ωνος (m.)—shirt, tunic
χλωρος—green
χρημα, -ατος (n.)—thing, possession (pl. money)
χρησμος, -ου (m.)—oracle
χρηστος—kind, good
χρονος, -ου (m.)—time
χρυσος, -ου (m.)—gold
χωρα, -ας (f.)—country

ψευδης—false
ψευδομαρτυρεω—give false witness
ψευδος, -ους (n.)—lie
ψευστης, -ου (m.)—liar
ψυχη, -ης (f.)—soul, life

ὡδε—here
ὡρα, -ας (f.)—hour
ὡς—as
ὡσπερ—as
ὡστε—so that

171

ENGLISH—GREEK VOCABULARY

(Genders of nouns are given in the Greek–English vocabulary only)

able (adj.)—δυνατος
able, I am—δυναμαι
abound—περισσευω
about—περι
abundantly—περισσον
according to—κατα
account—λογος
  (give account—λογον δουναι)
age—αιων
air—αιθηρ
akin—συγγενης
all—πας
allow—ἐαω
alone—μονος
alongside—παρα
although—καιπερ
always—ἀει
ancient—παλαιος
and—και
anger—ὀργη
angry, I am—ὀργιζομαι
animal—ζωον
announce—ἀγγελλω
answer—ἀποκρινομαι
apostle—ἀποστολος
armour—πανοπλιον
art—τεχνη
as—ὡς
ask (question)—ἐρωταω
assembly—ἐκκλησια
attendant—ὑπηρετης
authority—ἐξουσια

bad—κακος
bag—πηρα
baptism—βαπτισμα
Baptist—βαπτιστης
bark—φωνεω
beautiful—καλος
because—ὁτι, γαρ

become—γινομαι
bed—κλινη
before (place)—ἐνωπιον
begin—ἀρχομαι
beginning—ἀρχη
believe—πιστευω
beloved—ἀγαπητος
below—κατω
belt—ζωνη
bend—κλινω, ἐκκλινω
beseech—δεομαι
best—ἀριστος
big—μεγας
blessed—μακαριος
blood—αἱμα
boat—πλοιον
body—σωμα
book—βιβλιον
born, I am—γενναομαι
both—ἀμφοτεροι
boy—παις
bread—ἀρτος
bring—φερω
  (bring back—ἀναφερω)
bring forth (child)—τικτω
brother—ἀδελφος
but—ἀλλα, δε
by—ὑπο

call—καλεω
call (by name)—ἐπικαλεω
call out—φωνεω
can—δυναμαι
cancel—καταργεω
care for—θεραπευω
careful—ἀκριβης
carry—φερω
cast (net)—ἀμφιβαλλω
catastrophe—καταστροφη
cause—αἰτια

172

cease—παυομαι
chair—καθεδρα
child—παιδιον, τεκνον
circle—κυκλος
citizen—πολιτης
city—πολις
clear—φανερος
cloud—νεφελη
come—ἐρχομαι
come together—συνερχομαι
command—κελευω, παραγγελλω
commandment—ἐντολη,
                    παραγγελια
complete—τελεω
condemn—κατακρινω
confess—ὁμολογεω
conjecture—ὑπολαμβανω
contest—ἀγων
counsel—βουλη
country—χωρα
crocodile—κροκοδειλος
cross over—διαβαινω
crowd—ὀχλος, πληθος
crucify—σταυροω
cry out—κραζω, βοαω
custom—ἠθος

darkness—σκοτος
daughter—θυγατηρ
day—ἡμερα
dead—νεκρος
death—θανατος
deceive—πλαναω
defile—κοινοω
demon—δαιμονιον
desert (n.)—ἐρημος
desert (vb.)—καταλειπω
desire—ἐπιθυμεω
destroy—καταλυω
destruction—ἀπωλεια
devil—διαβολος
die—ἀποθνησκω
differ—διαφερομαι
dip—βαπτω
disciple—μαθητης
discuss—διαλεγομαι

disease—νοσημα
division—σχισμα
do—ποιεω, πρασσω
doctor—ἰατρος
dog—κυων
door—θυρα
draw near—ἐγγιζω
drink—πινω
drink up—καταπινω
dwell—παροικεω, οἰκεω
dysentery—δυσεντερια

each—ἑκαστος
ear—οὐς
ear (of corn)—σταχυς
early—πρωΐ
earth—γη
eat—ἐσθιω
eighth—ὀγδοος
elder—πρεσβυτερος
elsewhere—ἀλλαχου
end—τελος
enemy—ἐχθρος
enter—ἐμβαινω
error—πλανη
eternal—αἰωνιος
evangelist—εὐαγγελιστης
every—πας
exists—ὑπαρχει
eye—ὀφθαλμος

face—προσωπον
faithful—πιστος
fall—πιπτω
false—ψευδης
father—πατηρ
fault—παραπτωμα
fear (n.)—φοβος
fear (vb.)—φοβεομαι
field—ἀγρος
fifth—πεμπτος
fiftieth—πεντηκοστος
fight—μαχομαι
fill—πληροω
find—εὑρισκω
fire—πυρ

173

first—πρωτος
fish—ἰχθυς
five—πεντε
flame—φλοξ
flee—φευγω
flesh—σαρξ, κρεας
food—βρωμα
foolish—ἀφρων, μωρος
foot—πους
for (because)—γαρ
forgive—ἀφιημι
forgiveness—ἀφεσις
fourth—τεταρτος
free—ἐλευθερος
freedom—ἐλευθερια
freely—δωρεαν
friend—φιλος
from—ἀπο
fruit—καρπος
full—πληρης

gain—κερδος
game—ἀγων
garden—παραδεισος
garment—ἱματιον
generation—γενεα
Gentiles—ἐθνη
gift—δωρον
girl—κορη, παρθενος
give—διδωμι
glory—δοξα
go—βαινω, ἐρχομαι, πορευομαι
god—θεος
gold—χρυσος
good—ἀγαθος, καλος
gospel—εὐαγγελιον
govern—ἡγεμονευω
governor—ἡγεμων
grace—χαρις
great—μεγας
green—χλωρος
greet—ἀσπαζομαι
grief—λυπη
guard (n.)—φυλαξ
guard (vb.)—φυλασσω

hair—θριξ
half—ἡμισυ
hand—χειρ
happy—μακαριος
have—ἐχω
he—αὐτος
head—κεφαλη
heal—ἰαομαι
hear—ἀκουω
heart—καρδια
heaven—οὐρανος
help—βοηθεω
here—ἐνθαδε, ὡδε
Herod—Ἡρωδης
hidden—κρυπτος
hide—κρυπτω
high priest—ἀρχιερευς
hold—κρατεω
holy—ἁγιος
honour—τιμαω
hope—ἐλπις
hour—ὡρα
house—οἰκος
householder—οἰκοδεσποτης
how—ὁπως
human—ἀνθρωπινος
humble—ταπεινοω
hypocrite—ὑποκριτης

I—ἐγω
idol—εἰδωλον
if—εἰ
image—εἰκων, εἰδωλον
immediately—εὐθυς
immortal—ἀθανατος
impossible—ἀδυνατος
in—ἐν
infant—νηπιος
injure—βλαπτω, ἀδικεω
inn—πανδοχειον
innkeeper—πανδοχευς
innocent—ἀθωος
into—εἰς
is—ἐστι
it—αὐτο

jaw—γναθος
jealous—ζηλωτης
Jesus—'Ιησους
John—'Ιωαννης
Jordan—'Ιορδανης
judge (n.)—κριτης
judge (vb.)—κρινω
judgement—κριμα, κρισις
jump up—ἀναπηδαω
just—δικαιος
justify—δικαιοω

keep—τηρεω
kill—ἀποκτεινω
kind—χρηστος
king—βασιλευς
kingdom—βασιλεια
kinsman—συγγενης
know—γινωσκω
knowledge—γνωσις

lamb—ἀμνος
lamp—λαμπας
large—μακρος
last—ἐσχατος
law—νομος
lazy—ἀργος
lead—ἀγω
leader—ἡγεμων
leaf—φυλλον
learn—μανθανω
leave—λειπω, καταλειπω
left (hand)—ἀριστερος
leisure—σχολη
letter (of alphabet)—γραμμα
letter (epistle)—ἐπιστολη
liar—ψευστης
lie—ψευδος
life—ζωη, βιος
lift—αἰρω
lift up—ὑψοω
light—φως
like—ὁμοιος
lion—λεων
little—μικρος
live—ζαω
live with—παροικεω

long—μακρος
look at—βλεπω, θεωρεω
loosen—λυω
lord—κυριος
love (n.)—ἀγαπη
love (vb.)—ἀγαπαω, φιλεω

maiden—παρθενος
maidservant—παιδισκη
man—ἀνθρωπος, ἀνηρ
manifest—φανερος
manners—ἠθος
many—πολλοι
master—δεσποτης
measure—μετρον
meat—κρεας
mend—καταρτιζω
mercy—ἐλεος
messenger—ἀγγελος
middle—μεσος
miracle—σημειον, τερας
money—ἀργυριον, χρηματα
month—μην
mortal—θνητος
mother—μητηρ
mountain—ὀρος
mouth—στομα
move—κινεω
much—πολυς
murder (n.)—φονος
murder (vb.)—φονευω
must—(use δει)
mystery—μυστηριον

name (n.)—ὀνομα
name (vb.)—ἐπικαλεω
nation—γενος, ἐθνος
near—ἐγγυς
necessary, it is—δει
necessity—ἀναγκη
net—δικτυον
new—καινος, νεος
night—νυξ
ninth—ἐνατος
nobody—οὐδεις, μηδεις
not—οὐ, μη

175

obey—ύπακουω
officer—ύπηρετης
old—παλαιος
on—έν, έπι
one another—άλληλους
only—μονον
open—άνοιγω
opinion—δοξα
oracle—χρησμος
other—άλλος, έτερος
out of—έκ, έξ
owe—όφειλω
own—ίδιος
ox—βους

parable—παραβολη
parent—γονευς
peace—είρηνη
people—λαος, δημος
persuade—πειθω
pig—ύς
place (n.)—τοπος
place (vb.)—τιθημι
plan—βουλη
play-actor—ύποκριτης
poor—πτωχος
possible—δυνατος
power—δυναμις
practise—πρασσω
pray—δεομαι, προσευχομαι
preach—κηρυσσω
preach gospel—εύαγγελιζομαι
priest—ίερευς
prison—φυλακη
promise—έπαγγελια
prophet—προφητης
proselyte—προσηλυτης
prosper—εύτυχεω
province—έπαρχια
punish—τιμωρεω
pure—καθαρος
pursue—διωκω
put on—ένδυω

quickly—ταχεως, ταχυ

race, nation—γενος
read—άναγινωσκω
receive—λαμβανω, δεχομαι
rejoice—χαιρω, άγαλλιαομαι
relationship—όμιλια
religious—δεισιδαιμων
remain—μενω
repent—μετανοεω
report—άναγγελλω
resurrection—άναστασις
return—ύπαγω
reverence—εύσεβεω
reward—μισθος
right (hand)—δεξιος
righteous—δικαιος
righteousness—δικαιοσυνη
river—ποταμος
road—όδος
robber—ληστης
rouse—έγειρω
rule—άρχη

sabbath—σαββατον
sacred—ίερος
sacrifice—θυσια
salt (n.)—άλας
salt (vb.)—άλιζω
salvation—σωτηρια
save—σωζω
saviour—σωτηρ
say—λεγω, φημι
school—σχολη
scribe—γραμματευς
scriptures—γραφαι
sea—θαλασσα
seat—καθεδρα
second—δευτερος
see—βλεπω, θεωρεω, όραω
seed—σπερμα
seek—ζητεω
seize—άρπαζω, κρατεω
self—αύτος
sell—άποδιδομαι
send—πεμπω, άποστελλω
servant—δουλος
serve—λατρευω

176

seventh—ἕβδομος
shadow—σκια
she—αὐτη
sheep—προβατον
shepherd—ποιμην
shine—λαμπω
shirt—χιτων
short—μικρος
sign—σημειον
silent, be—σιωπαω, σιγαω
silver—ἀργυριον
sin (n.)—ἁμαρτια
sin (vb.)—ἁμαρτανω
sinner—ἁμαρτωλος
sit—καθιζω
six—ἑξ
skill—τεχνη
slave—δουλος
sleep, go to—κοιμαομαι
smack—τυπτω
small—μικρος
snatch—ἁρπαζω
so, thus—οὑτως
so that—ὡστε
soldier—στρατιωτης
someone—τις
son— υἱος
soul—ψυχη
sound—φωνη, ἠχος
sow—σπειρω
speak—λαλεω, λεγω
spend (time)—διατριβω
spirit—πνευμα
spoil—μωραινω
stand—ἱστημι
star—ἀστηρ
steal—κλεπτω
stop—παυω (tr.),
   παυομαι (intr.)
stranger—προσηλυτης
strife—ἐρις
strike—τυπτω
strong—ἰσχυρος
strong, I am—ἰσχυω
student—μαθητης
suffer—πασχω

suffering—παθημα, **παθος**
synagogue—**συναγωγη**

table—τραπεζα
take—λαμβανω
talent—ταλαντον
tax-collector—τελωνης
teach—διδασκω
teacher—διδασκαλος
temple—ἱερον
temptation—πειρασμος
ten—δεκα
tent—σκηνη
tenth—δεκατος
terrify—φοβεω
testament—διαθηκη
that (conj.)—ὁτι
then—τοτε
they—αὐτοι
thief—κλεπτης
thing—χρημα
think—νομιζω, **ὑπολαμβανω**
third—τριτος
thought—νοημα
throw—βαλλω
thus—οὑτως
time—καιρος, χρονος
to—προς
tongue—γλωσσα
tooth—ὀδους
touch—ἁπτομαι
tree—δενδρον
trial—πειρασμος
tribe—ἐθνος
true—ἀληθης
trumpet—σαλπιγξ
truth—ἀληθεια
tunic—χιτων
turn—στρεφω
turn away—ἀποστρεφω
turn out—ἐκβαλλω
twelve—δωδεκα
twenty—εἰκοσι
two—δυο
tyranny—τυραννις

under—ὑπο
understand—συνιημι
unskilled—ἀπειρος

vain—ματαιος
vainly—ματην
village—κωμη
vineyard—ἀμπελων
vision—ὁραμα
voice—φωνη

wake (keep awake)—γρηγορεω
walk—περιπατεω
warm—θερμος
wash—λουω
watch—τηρεω, φυλασσω
water—ὑδωρ
way—ὁδος
we—ἡμεις
weak—ἀσθενης
well—καλως, εὐ
when—ὁτε
where—ὁπου
white—λευκος
who—ὁς

who?—τις ;
wicked—πονηρος
wife—γυνη
will—θελημα
wind—ἀνεμος, πνευμα
winter—χειμων
wisdom—σοφια
wise—σοφος
wish—θελω, βουλομαι
with—μετα, συν
witness—μαρτυρεω
woman—γυνη
wonderful—θαυμαστος
word—λογος, ῥημα
work (n.)—ἐργον
work (vb.)—ἐργαζομαι
workman—ἐργατης
world—κοσμος
worthy—ἀξιος
write—γραφω
writing—γραφη

year—ἐτος
you—συ (sing.), ὑμεις (pl.)
young man—νεανιας